A Million Fireflies

Mali Phonpadith

A Million Fireflies

synergy press

A Million Fireflies

Library of Congress
Cataloging – in – Publishing Data

Phonpadith, Mali.
A Million Fireflies
Life Journey/ Mali Phonpadith – 1st ed.

p.cm
Includes references
ISBN – 13: 978-0-9802209-4-0
ISBN – 10: 0-9802209-4-7

1. Phonpadith, Mali, date.
2. Women – United States – Biography.
3. Lao – American – Biography.
4. A Collection of Original Poetry.

FIRST EDITION
Published by Synergy Press
Book Designer: Norasack Design
Photographer: Jhason Abuan

Synergy Press books may be purchased in bulk for educational, business, or sales promotional use. For more information please write:
order@synergypressonline.com

A Million Fireflies:
Table of Contents

Dedication

A Million Fireflies is dedicated to the beautiful souls who graced my life and offered me a sense of wonder, joy, hope, passion, love and peace. Though they are no longer with me physically, my greatest reward for publishing this book is to honor them and allow their legacy to live on forever.

Sivone Phonpadith, my father, was the kindest, most generous soul I have ever known.

Christopher Meehan, a soul mate who will travel with me through eternity, introduced me to the real meaning of love and changed my life forever.

Chester Saykhamphone, whose smile will always be part of my journey, reminded me to keep my inner child present and alive.

Wendell Mac McCarty, who was also my father in my heart, taught me that I can do and be anything I want in life.

Rafael Beckford, my best friend, taught me unconditional love and how to share the depth of my soul without expectation or fear of judgment.

My life is brilliant and full of beautiful colors because of you, all of you

✹ ✹ ✹

Introduction
How to Release a Million Fireflies

The title of this book came to me one cold, bitter January night as I tried to fall asleep in a hospital room on an uncomfortable couch next to my mother, who had just undergone spinal surgery. Over the previous five hours, I had heard every second of the clock beat against my own heart. I felt the familiar heaviness of an elephant on my chest, the elephant of grief I'd grown to know intimately over the past five years. Many times, she had prepared to leave me, but each time she was ready to set forth on a different journey, something in my life forced her to stay. Now, I felt her full weight again and I could hardly recall a time when I didn't live with her resting upon me.

In these lonely, burdened hours, with the sound of hospital monitors as background music, I reflected on my book. I had been working on a collection of my written works for more than three years, but something always kept me from moving forward and publishing it. I looked up at the sky through the window and saw stars flickering. Suddenly, I had visions of fireflies. My mother slept, and as I listened to the sound of her breath, all I wanted was to remember a time when the world was full of butterflies and fireflies, when my greatest joy was chasing grasshoppers in the backyard of my childhood home. I remember imagining that each firefly I captured somehow found its way inside my heart. I believed that in a moment of need, all the fireflies I ever caught and released would light up and lead me toward the right path in life.

So much has changed since the simple days of my childhood. Grief, fear, deception, loss, love, anxiety, joy, hope, a bleeding heart, a tested will, clouded instincts – each of these painful components of life have culminated in a thick, elephant-like skin on top of the tiny child's heart that was once wide open and filled with fireflies.

In that hospital room, I watched my mother try to keep her pain and anxiety to herself, to try and carry her burden alone. I realized that I have handled my life's many challenges in the same manner. I carefully placed each emotional trauma deep inside my own heart and prayed it would somehow sort itself out. The layers of my grief eventually wove themselves together, creating a thick skin to protect my tender heart.

This is why I had not published my book. Each piece of poetry and prose commemorated another layer, and I had grown dependent on them – as much as I had grown to need that benign, sad and comforting elephant. You see, my writings cushioned the pain. If I gathered them all, looked at them all at once, all together, and then released them to the world, I might lose that safety net. Sure, it was a painful net in which to lie, but it was a familiar one.

And yet, somewhere within me, I felt the flutter of tiny gossamer wings pressing against all my senses. I couldn't help but wish to shift my attention back to a time and place when grasshoppers, butterflies and fireflies were plentiful and within reach. How much fun it was to dance with them amongst the tall grass and emulate their free spiritedness. As a child, I ran without care. As an adult, I watch every step, always trying to find the path that will provide me safety, that will be least likely to yield yet another painful loss.

Yet, I must stop and remind myself that my life is not a dress rehearsal. I am alive today, and there are extraordinary people and things right here on the road I am traveling. I must unburden this heart, peel off each layer one by one and overcome that fear of loss to uncover my buried core. Underneath all of this protection, there is still a child within me, a little girl who lived life so fully, who grabbed hold of all those fireflies, appreciated them and then released them one by one into the open sky. She wasn't afraid of anything. She trusted that everything was just right with the world.

That night in my mother's hospital room, one in a long line of hospital rooms I have known in recent years, I listened to her heartbeat and to what my own heart had to tell me. My loved ones and their legacies lit up the world for me as a child and their warm glow tugs me out of myself now. The spirits and voices of the many people I have loved deeply and lost too soon are the fireflies I have captured and held in my heart for safekeeping. They are alive inside of me!

I am finally ready to release the million fireflies. I have kept them to myself for too long. They have taught me everything I need to know to become a firefly myself. I must trust that they have led me to exactly where I am meant to be. As I release them, they also set me free to spread my wings and light up the night sky.

As you read, I hope you will embrace them, for they have experienced tragedy, grief, fear and pain, but they now shine brighter than ever before.

PART I

ELEPHANTS AND FIREFLIES

"Fly"

Remember the smell of honeydew –
A time when all that mattered was me and you?
My sundress flowing with each chase of a grasshopper
[1] Paw laughing and yelling toward Mai :
"Just let her be – there is nothing that can stop her!"

The stillness of the air
I created the tossing of each strand of hair
Held conversations
with twinkling lights upon open skies
I knew then, I was born to fly.

It never took too long to see your curious glance
Approving every step of my crazy, spontaneous and clumsy dance
A touch of the shoulder and all my fears went away
I feel that touch as frequently as I feel the wind these days.

Remember the calm before each lightning storm?
The peace within my core shelters me; keeps me warm
I held back my emotions for so many years
Did not understand the importance
of releasing each loving tear
Display my heart; release my fears
I'm grateful for second chances
Grateful for what has led me here

Vivid colors dance around me
Earth, Sea, Sky
I know now, it is time to fly.

[1] "Paw" and "Mai" are Lao words for "Dad" and Mom."

Land of a Million Elephants

Laos, the land of my birth, is a landlocked country, quiet in its demeanor, yet resilient and proud. A landscape of rugged mountains, a climate of monsoon and drought, and a people embattled, exploited and enlightened, occupy the heart of Central Southeast Asia. Though modern-day Laos has become a popular travel destination, it was once caught in the middle of the Vietnam War. Beneath the surface of natural beauty and graceful people is a recent history of grief, unhealed wounds and hidden landmines.

Laos is the homeland I fled with my family at the tender age of four, half asleep, in the dark of night, across the Mekong River, riding on my grandmother's hip.

When I was born, the Vietnam War had been officially declared over, but it still raged in Laos. The North Vietnamese and its communist leader, Pathet Lao, emerged victorious during the year of my birth and quickly led a movement to spread communism throughout the Southeast region that year. Growing up, my grandmother and father often told me stories of this time in our lives – including those of family members and friends killed by the massive bombings that terrorized our home.

My family lived in the city of Thakhek, in the Khammouane province. Khammouane is located in the center of the country, in the upper half of the panhandle over which so much devastation was spread, with the Vietnam border to its east. The North Vietnamese army established the infamous Ho Chi Minh Trail here as a route for supplies and troops. This caused the sky to rain bombs, and the people were forced to choose sides.

From the air, the United States conducted massive warfare as they tried to stop the spread of communism. According to *The Guardian*, "Laos was hit by an average of one B-52 bomb load every eight minutes, 24 hours a day, between 1964 and 1973." That's more bombs than were dropped in all of World War II, giving my homeland the distinction of being the most heavily-bombed country in the world. Eighty million of these bombs failed to explode and now rest, half buried and lethal, in the hillsides and forests. Despite the biggest bombing campaign in world history, the effort failed to prevent the Communist Party from defeating the royal monarchy of Laos, the kingdom of Lan Xang, which means, "Land of a Million Elephants." As the new government took over, the old ways of living changed, as if all million elephants were ceremoniously led to slaughter, grief-stricken and broken-hearted. Though my father, Sivone, spoke often of the war and the events that led to it, he rarely talked with me about the actual occupation. It was too difficult for him to recount the painful, specific details of what he personally witnessed and endured. The little he did share was enough to help me understand why he was always worried about our safety and stability.

Before the Pathet Lao regime took over, my father worked for the royal government of Laos as a humanitarian. Therefore, he and his colleagues were prime targets. They were blacklisted, and my father burned all documents linking him to the old government. He buried his uniform and prayed he would not be discovered.

My father, like so many others who had been unable to flee the country early on, was eventually interned in a remote, disease-ridden camp for "re-education." Had the guards known of his close affiliation with the previous government, he would most likely have been killed. The re-education camps were called *Samana*, and their purpose was to break the will of the old regime loyalists and instill fear of the new regime in all men. My father was in and out of *Samana* for a couple of months. What he witnessed there would haunt him for the rest of his life.

My father always played by the rules. It was his way of getting by in life. He was mistreated in the camps like all the rest, but unlike many of his colleagues and close friends, who defied the new teachings and were tortured and often brutally killed, my father always had the great gift of "keeping the peace," a trait that I inherited.

When he was not being "re-educated," he dedicated all of his time to plotting our escape. Along with my grandmother and mother, he had three very young daughters to consider in this grand exodus. It took three years, but through secret letters and encrypted telegrams to relatives living in Thailand, my father was able to coordinate and execute an escape plan.

He negotiated an exchange with a family that lived along the Mekong River – his land and worldly possessions for their boat. He had papers drafted and, with a little cash exchange, was able to get official documents stating that he and his family were traveling south to the Laotian city of Savannakhet to visit ailing relatives. We would need this precaution if we got caught and stopped by Pathet Lao's armed forces.

Then one morning before dawn, we set out on foot for our new boat. My father told me later that he could hear sirens in the distance. Although he and my mother had given us girls each a small dose of sleeping medication, he feared we would make noise and be discovered, captured or killed. But he was determined to keep us moving forward. We continued until we got to the riverbank.

My grandmother often recounts her experience of that day. She has told me many times of her anxiety and deep sadness during that journey. She feared for her life. She feared the unknown future that awaited her if she actually survived. She was heartbroken from having to say good-bye to the only home she had known in her 53 years of life. She felt paralyzed, but her soul simply knew to follow her feet. Like sad elephants, we were leaving the homeland we knew, carrying nothing with us but our loved ones and our memories, which only served to make our hearts heavier.

We made it across the Mekong River, the border between Laos and Thailand, and came ashore at the exact coordinates my father mapped out. Our relatives were there to greet us in a produce truck. We all got in the back and hid until we reached the home of my father's uncle, who had lived in Thailand for many years and become a citizen. We stayed with his family for a couple of weeks until they could work out a plan to get us safe entrance into a refugee camp in Ubon, Thailand.

Again, we went in the middle of night. Because of the civil unrest in Laos and all over Southeast Asia, the refugee camps were completely full. Space, supplies and aid workers were scarce, and the camps were not "officially" sheltering any more families. We were going to have to sneak in. Our uncle drove us as close as he could get to the refugee camp without the guards hearing his truck.

The story becomes a bit fuzzy here. I don't remember any fireflies showing up to guide us, though my mother does. I just have a vague nightmare of sobs and feet running with only flashlights to cut through the darkness. My grandmother recounts how she, my father and his uncle shoveled dirt and created a ditch underneath the barbed-wired fence. One by one, each family member crawled under that fence – including my mother, who was seven months pregnant with my brother – and we made it into the safe haven of the camp. Once we were in, they could not force us out.

I don't have a single memory of the refugee camp. Neither does my older sister, Mina, who was six years old at the time. Perhaps the chaos was too much for our young minds to bear. I only have vivid images, created in my imagination from stories my parents and grandmother told me. According to my grandmother, the camp consisted of thousands of tents, most of which housed multiple families. Some had mattresses; others had only blankets and pillows. Many people suffered from sickness and malnutrition. Some of the refugees roamed around grief-stricken over lost or displaced loved ones. There were also "foreigners," people who worked there and spoke languages my family could not understand, asking us to take off our shirts for measurements and sticking needles into our arms. Everything was new and alarming.

Our family was very fortunate. We were there for less than a year before Davies Unitarian Church sponsored our family to come to the United States as permanent residents. Like fugitive fireflies, we escaped from the lost Land of a Million Elephants.

I was born in March of 1975, when Laos was still officially (though precariously) under the rule of a million smiling elephants. Perhaps blessed by those elephants, I came into the world quickly and peacefully. My mother, Keonoukane, sat on the floor of her home, held onto the door knob, and with a single push, there I was – quiet and full of smiles.

Four years later, in 1979, we fled Laos, frantic and scared, as if being herded by protective elephants out of danger. What I have learned about that time in our lives taught me many important life lessons, and those realizations flicker and light my path like fireflies. I learned that, with deep love of family and the will to live a

brilliant and peaceful life, you can make anything happen.
I learned of my parents' strength and determination. I learned of
my grandmother's bravery. I learned that even during the darkest
nights and most difficult circumstances, faith, hope and love can
get us through any of life's challenges.

Though I have not lived in Laos since I was a child, it is my
homeland, and its million elephants are part of me. Throughout
my life, they have symbolically shown up to cushion any blows.
They come to sit and rest with me for as long as I need and then
nudge me to the edge of each new Mekong I must cross.

America, my home for the last 30 years, is where a million fireflies
have led me. They remain my guiding light through each dark
night and teach me how to flutter my wings and shine for the
benefit of the world. I have not returned to Laos. That is a Mekong
I must cross in the near future…

"Crossing the Ocean"

Night skies whisper a familiar tune
taking me back to days I barely recall.
I was a child transformed – an adult before sentences formed to escape my lips.
I arrived to greet winter storms – so foreign to my eyes and spirit.
I shiver to think what would have become if I never made it to find you?

If dawn had arrived too soon for me to cross,
how safe would my haven have been on the other side?
I did not have any corners left to turn,
only forward ... taking fearful, determined strides to claim a new home.
You – so far in the distance – waited anxiously with open arms.

Night skies now sing a familiar song,
pondering when I will be ready
to place my bare feet upon her soil once more.
I am still that child – now an adult who speaks too many sentences out loud.
Wishing to return to dance alongside her tropical breeze,
I tremble to think how my world would be if she never forced me free,
crossing the ocean with nothing but a fiery spirit to guide me
through open seas.

✳ ✳ ✳

Fireflies in America:
A Heroic Effort to Survive

I once asked my mother if she remembered any fireflies during our trek from Laos to Thailand, and she responded with certainty, "Of course there were fireflies. They greeted us every evening around dusk. They were also there when we arrived safely inside the refugee camp." That's not surprising to me. Fireflies have appeared to shine light onto my world during some of the most traumatic and meaningful moments of my life. Why should that journey be an exception?"

When we arrived in the United States, it was wintertime in Washington, D.C. In Laos, we had never experienced such cold temperatures and we had no real concept of snow. My grandmother confessed that she was worried she had left a war-torn country only to enter a bitter, cold hell. Although she was fascinated by the beauty of white fluffiness falling from the sky, she was so fearful, disoriented and lonely that the beautiful white world felt more like a barren country blanketing her true essence. She could not breathe easily for months.

Mai and Paw [2], also grieving the loss of their beloved homeland, experienced a howling emptiness in their souls. Left with little defense against the bitter chill, they constantly felt physically and spiritually broken and lost.

When I think of that transition period, I feel a deep ache in my heart for them. How were they ever able to cope with so much change and loss? How were they able to feel any sense of calm and peace when they couldn't express their concerns, desires and needs to people who spoke a language they could not comprehend? My parents' new "normal" life was punctuated with sleepless nights and anxiety.

---

[2] "Mai" and "Paw" are the Lao words for "Mom" and "Dad."

In those early days, Davies Unitarian Church, the Maryland-based church that sponsored our immigration, found some government funding. This, combined with support from Davies members, was enough to house us in a tiny apartment in a low-income housing community in the southeastern part of Washington, D.C. Our family of seven shared a three-bedroom apartment with two other immigrant families, one from Vietnam and one from Cambodia. Each family had its own room. We conserved food and ate it sparingly. The cold followed us indoors through cracks in several of the windows.

Life in the big city was deafening with the noise of police cars, ambulances, neighbors screaming and fighting, and the general hustle and bustle of life. My grandmother once referred to the chaos as the sound of new elephants roaring. Stress, pain, sorrow, homesickness and fear of our unknown future were daunting.

Then, one day in early spring, we all went for a walk around the neighborhood and spotted a cluster of fireflies, the first we'd seen in our new country. Mai was filled with hope. She didn't believe fireflies existed here, because she assumed that the United States was perpetually cold. She was thrilled to witness new signs of life and light as the temperature grew warmer. Perhaps this place wouldn't be so unfamiliar and unpleasant after all.

My parents began to feel better as spring buzzed and burst onto the D.C. scene. With willing and optimistic spirits, they followed the advice of friends from the church and learned the new daily rituals necessary for life in the US. Eventually, all of our paperwork was processed, and Mina and I could start pre-school and kindergarten. Every new day accumulated more forward momentum. My parents slept better. My grandmother was able to meditate and breathe more freely. Time began its healing work, starting with the surprise appearance of the fireflies, and we moved along on the springtime tide.

About a year later, our church friends helped us rent an apartment in Marlow Heights, Maryland. They helped my father find work nearby at a car dealership. Since he did not speak any English, the only job he qualified for was the janitor position, but he was ecstatic to have work and an opportunity to earn money.

The dealership was about five miles from our apartment, so the church scrounged up a bicycle for my father. Paw rode that bicycle back and forth to work for more than a year – in sunshine, rain and snowstorms. He worked 10- to 12-hour days, six days a week, and always requested over-time to get extra money. On weekends, he did odd jobs – painting fences, planting trees and flowers, and cutting grass for members of the church to save for our household needs. While he appreciated the immense generosity we'd experienced, my father worked hard to reclaim his sense of independence. He wanted to earn his own way and no longer wished to rely on the church, or government "hand-outs," as he called them.

My mother eventually found work at a local bakery within walking distance. Because of her limited English, they could only offer her a dishwasher position. She worked from 8:00 a.m. until 6:00 p.m. and came home with wrinkled hands from the dishwater.

My parents both made minimum wage, and whenever they could get extra hours, they gladly accepted the work. Though they worked with their hands, the work was restorative, and my parents were thrilled to have something to occupy their minds and spirits besides worry. A small portion of their paychecks went to food and the rest to savings. Within a year, Paw bought a little orange station wagon off the used lot for $500. Instead of walking everywhere, we started riding to the grocery store, and my father retired his bicycle. With the advent of the orange station wagon and a whole new way of getting around, my parents were able to work more.

Paw got a second job, cleaning another dealership at night, and Mai found work as a hotel housekeeper at J.W. Marriott in Washington, D.C., where she still works today. All the tips my mother collected went toward groceries. The rest was for bills and savings.

In 1987, seven years after we moved to the United States, my parents put a down payment on a single-family home in Upper Marlboro, Maryland. Paw built a beautiful garden in the backyard, and it was there where I danced many nights with thousands of happy and brilliant fireflies, always remembering the fireflies we saw that day only months after our arrival, whose warm glow heralded the end of winter and the beginning of our new lives.

Elephant Memory:
How We Keep Laos Alive in Our Hearts

Though my family had to leave Laos behind, its spirit permeated our childhood home – in the form of its most sacred animal. There were a million elephants in our house (at least it seemed like it); they were everywhere. In fact, they seemed to inhabit the place as much as we did. There were ceramic elephant statues of varying shapes and sizes displayed in a glass showcase in our dining room.

My mother purchased silk screen prints of these majestic, sacred creatures, which she framed and placed on our walls. And my grandmother often entertained us all with Laotian fairytales that portrayed the magic and power of elephants.

As a little girl, I learned that elephants are considered sacred in Laos. Countless ancient Lao tales involve kingdoms at war to control people and land. The mighty elephants, strong and resilient, yet gentle and nurturing, led good warriors to safety and peace in new lands. The stronger and wiser the elephant, the more victorious her chosen warriors would be.

"The Lao people are like elephants," my grandmother once told me. "They know the ins and outs of the land, yet they are brave and resilient enough to explore new territory." She described our family as a herd of elephants crossing the ocean into new lands. We often felt lost, but we always stayed close and connected, like elephants crossing a rugged landscape, trunks linked to tails.

In fact, elephants exhibit many of the traits needed for survival when the world suffers upheaval and people are displaced. They rely on a well-structured social order, with females at the center of activity and stability. Biologically, they are built to stand for long periods of time without tiring. They can swim well and are able to cross river boundaries that would be daunting to pursuers (like the Mekong). They make up for poor eyesight with a sixth sense: empathy. Elephants can recognize themselves in the mirror, an ability found in very few animals besides humans. This self-recognition is a necessary precursor to being able to feel for others, which is crucial to survival in a world which continues to suffer upheaval. Seeing, feeling for and helping one another does not prevent suffering, but it does help to ease it.

In the midst of our upheaval, my parents wanted us to assimilate into the American culture, but they also believed in preserving our traditions. At home, my siblings and I primarily spoke Lao to them and Grandma. They also learned English vicariously through us, asking us to share what we learned in school at the dinner table. At these times, we spoke in English, sharing stories from books we were reading as well as facts about animals we were studying and American history.

While our dinner-table conversations revolved around our new world, the *meals* tasted of our roots in Laos. My mother and grandmother prepared every meal from scratch. Grandma took care of breakfast and afterschool snacks. Mai cooked all our dinners. Each night, our home would be filled with the rich aromas of lemongrass, ginger, mints and cilantro. And there was always a wide spread with several dishes, ranging from spicy noodle bowls, to stir fry, to papaya salad, to barbecued meats, to bamboo stew. Lao food is very communal; everything is shared. Throughout the meal, the many different dishes are passed down the table from one person to the next. In this way, my family stayed connected as we ate. We talked about everything under the sun and moon over dinner for all those years. Many nights were filled with laughter, and on other nights we sat quietly – depending on our moods and the stresses of the day.

When I was a teenager, Mai declared our evening meals to be sacred and made it clear that they were not optional.

"I don't care if you guys want to order food or eat at different times for breakfast or lunch," she told us. "But we will eat a home-cooked meal for dinner and we will wait to eat it together." This shared meal was extremely important to my parents because it was often the only time of the day they had to connect with each other and their kids. It was a way to protect our bond as a family, so attendance was mandatory for the entire family – me, my parents, Grandma, my older sister, Mina, my younger sister, Lola, and my brother, Soudara. Because Mai and Paw each worked two to three jobs, my siblings and I often snacked before dinner, but we always waited until they got home, stopped whatever we were doing (usually homework) and gathered around the dinner table together. Sometimes, this would not happen until 9:00 or 10:00 p.m. But we waited.

Our connection to our heritage was vital to my parents; they wanted their children to learn and understand Lao traditions, speak the language fluently, and practice the spiritual and cultural rituals. So, Paw and Mai became involved with the Lao Hwormit Association, a local Lao group created to keep our small local community of immigrant families from feeling so alone as we adjusted to America. My father became an active member and served as secretary or treasurer for many years. We grew up balancing the religion of our homeland with the predominant religion of our adopted country. Because of the loving support from Davies Unitarian Church, we participated in Sunday school programs and learned the Unitarian viewpoints of God and religion. Having friends at church and plenty of activities was a great way for us kids to socialize, but my parents felt it was important to balance this exposure to Christianity with the Buddhism of their own childhoods. It was not difficult to reconcile the two traditions; the core teachings of love are very similar. The rituals, sacred spaces and basic practices were different, but this was fascinating to me. In fact, balancing the two religions helped me keep a clear focus on their commonality, the element both groups said was most important – love.

There are many different types of Buddhism. The three most popular sects are Mahayana, Theravada and Varjayana. My parents learned Theravada, which is practiced in South- and Southeast-Asia, including Laos. Theravada rituals mark most of the big moments in life – including birth, marriage, and death.

There were several Buddhist temples in the D.C. area, but very few were of the Theravada sect. The sacred language of Theravada Buddhism, *Pali*, stems from the ancient Indic language of Sanskrit. So, we could go to the other temples that used *Pali* if we just wanted to recite the chants, but not all of them did. And none used the specific Theravada rituals.

My parents wanted more for us; they wanted us to have a sense of belonging. And having arrived in the United States feeling so lost and isolated from their roots, they wanted it for themselves too. So, they made it part of their legacy to help the Lao association create a sacred, authentic space for immigrants from our homeland to worship. It took more than 12 years to collect enough money, but the Lao community came together and eventually funded the establishment of a Lao Buddhist temple in Catlett, Virginia.

The temple was completed in July of 1993. Spread over 50 acres, the beautiful, rustic grounds include the main temple where larger ceremonies and rituals take place, a house where the monks sleep and a few meditation buildings where anyone can spend time with their own thoughts and prayers. There is a man-made pond where water lilies grow wild and colorful carp swim freely. Beyond these main buildings are rows upon rows of memorial and burial sites for our loved ones. My father's ashes now roam freely on the grounds of the sacred space he helped to create.

My parents took us there for the major holidays and festivals. Paw was not a deeply religious man. Spirituality mattered more to him, so the rituals were not as important. But he wanted us to believe in something greater than ourselves without pushing a particular religious view. My mother and grandmother were more inclined to participate in the rituals and blessings of the Buddhist teachings, and so my siblings and I had a nice balance of both approaches. We were not forced to memorize Bible verses or Buddhist chants and meditations.

The only area where they were truly inflexible was temple etiquette. Take off your shoes before entering the main temple; bow three times to greet the sacred spirits; listen intently to the blessings being spoken and offered by the monks; bow three times upon leaving the sacred grounds of the temple. These are signs of respect, and that was not up for discussion.

Having the Lao Buddhist temple helped us better define what life as a "Lao-American" was all about: working hard and doing the best we could to assimilate while staying connected to our roots. At the temple, we could make friends who were just as lost as we were in this new land. We came together as community and continued our sacred traditions, such as paying respects to the gods and all the sacred spirits during the water festival by throwing holy water while having parades and enjoying other fun activities. And my parents and grandmother reunited with friends and relatives, many of whom they believed had perished during the war.

The Lao Buddhist temple allowed us to feel as though we were visiting our homeland. The temple grounds and activities are not designed for luxury but rather to communicate an authentic feel. The architecture is similar to the traditional Lao temples and the majority of people who go there are Lao-Americans, Thai, Vietnamese and Cambodian-Americans who practice the same sect of Buddhism. During the major annual festivals, vendors set up stands to sell food, drinks and other goods – just as if they were conducting business in one of the outdoor markets in Laos. People dressed in traditional Lao attire and speaking the Lao language show a sense of pride in our heritage. The aromatic smells of lemongrass barbeque chicken, traditional Lao papaya salad and spicy noodle soup mingle with the sounds of traditional Lao music, screaming children and laughing adults. And if you listen closely over all that noise and celebration at the temple my family helped build, you can hear the roaring of a million triumphant elephants.

"Eastward"

I long for repatriation of the soul
to a homeland I cannot remember.
In memory, the soil goes untouched by these hands,
The water never wraps itself
between these fingers, these toes.
Not to recall the beauty of my birthplace
leaves me incomplete.
I want for a place to call my home.
I feel safe within the walls of this land,
yet I cannot ignore the whispers of my name
on faraway winds, touching the weathervane of memory,
Pointing me eastward.

The Inheritance of my Grandmother's Spirit

My grandmother woke from her nap and sat up on the couch. I bent down to kiss her cheek. She was visiting me in D.C. for the week, and I came home to eat with her with on my lunch break. Grandma often requested quality time with me. She lived with my parents, but she spent most of her days alone. My parents worked, and her grandchildren had their own lives. She entertained herself by working in the garden and watching telenovellas on the Hispanic stations. She must be fluent in Spanish, having watched them for 30 years, but I don't know that for sure, because we still communicate together in Lao, except for when she surprises me with an occasional and endearing "Love you."

My grandmother, Khamkong, was born in 1927. In Laos, women of her class rarely had the opportunity to pursue higher education, if any at all. And her father needed his girls to work on the farm and in the rice fields. But when my grandmother was 11 years old, she decided that she wanted to learn, even if that meant lying to her father and siblings. She told her family that she was going to her aunt's home each day to learn how to farm. Instead, she headed straight to class and learned how to read and write. She lied for a couple of years until her father discovered the truth. He didn't like that she lied but he allowed her to continue through grade school, when they would need her to help support the household. My grandmother was the only person in her entire family who was literate and knew basic mathematics. She spent the rest of her time on the farm, in the fields and selling food at the local street markets.

The fourth child among five siblings, my grandmother had such a strong work ethic, and a persistent and stubborn nature, that people often mistook her for the eldest. And Khamkong was her father's favorite. Because she preferred the outdoors and didn't like staying home as much as her sisters, she didn't learn many household chores until after she was married to my grandfather.

But that afternoon when I came home for lunch, I couldn't tell she'd been a late bloomer in the kitchen. She had prepared a feast: papaya salad, Lao sticky rice and chicken stir fry. I laughed and told her she was spoiling me and that I appreciated how special she was making me feel.

✳✳✳

"*Nang*," she said.[3] "You *are* special. There has always been something about you that draws people in. You were born with a golden hue, a birthmark on the top of your head. It was cone-shaped. To me, it resembled a crown. From the moment you were born, there was a different energy about you. You entered the world peacefully and with a lot of joy."

She recounted a story that I'd heard several times before – the story of my grand entrance into this world. My mother was alone the morning she gave birth to me, squatting in the threshold of our family's home in Laos. My father was at work. And Grandma had gone out for salt. In Laos, most women bore their children in their homes, assisted by their mothers, sisters and friends as midwives. My mother woke up that Monday morning with contractions, so Grandma knew I would soon be entering the world, and they would need salt for a warm bath to clean my body once the umbilical cord was cut and secured.

A few minutes after Grandma left, a strong contraction almost knocked my mother to the floor. From the window, she could see my grandmother walking down the street, but the contractions were too painful for her to muster up a call for help.

She sank down with her back against the front door to wait for the contractions to subside. Her water broke. In an effort to raise herself off the floor, she reached behind her head, grabbed the doorknob and pulled. And I popped right out! Mai was astonished it was that quick and easy. When my grandmother arrived home less than an hour later, there I was, smiling at her from my mother's arms, umbilical cord and all.

"It's always been that simple and easy with you, *nang*," Grandma told me, laughing at the memory. "And the villagers, young and old, were constantly stopping by to visit with you, more than they would with other children. Most of them wanted to hold you and spend time just playing with you. I'd never seen anything like it. But we welcomed it. Your father nicknamed you 'Thu-Thu' because your cheeks were so squeezable and you were very easy going. You went with anyone who wanted to carry you."

---

[3] "*Nang*" is the Lao word for "darling."

But Grandma didn't think the nickname was appropriate for my life journey. "I knew you would grow out of the chubby phase," she said. "I preferred a name that would be more reflective of the energy that came with you. I wanted to call you Sunay."

"What does Sunay mean?" I asked.

She stroked my hair and gently caressed the right side of my forehead, where she remembered my birthmark being. "It means 'charisma' in Lao. The energy force you came with still lives so brilliantly inside of you. Sunay is the perfect word for you still today."

She paused and took a sip of her tea. I continued to take slow bites in silence, while I wrapped my head and heart around what she was telling me.

"It's a great responsibility you carry, my dear child," she continued. "Everyone has and will continue to rely on you for so many things. Even I find myself doing that to you. At times, I know it feels burdensome, yet it is who you have been created to be."

I sat there staring at her, trying not to cry. She looked into my eyes, and without exchanging a word, she got confirmation that her words struck me at my core. "It's a gift, *nang*," she said. "Your capacity to hold so much love as well as pain. It's all a gift."

This capacity for feeling and the strength to bear it runs like a strong, deep river through my family. My grandmother possesses this capacity to hold both the enormous joy and pain of life. As a child, she had an unwavering determination, and that spirit has never left her. Paradoxically, she also has the ability to be deeply vulnerable. She does not share her emotions easily, so as a child, I truly believed she was made of stone, always so stoic and unyielding. I would later come to understand that while she is tough on the outside, she is also extremely sensitive to other people's opinions and judgments.

Her evident strength, drive and independence drove my grandfather to fall in love with her. When they met, she was 22 years old and he was 25. He was a soldier, and she sold noodles at the market near the military base where he was stationed.

My grandfather, who I only know as Pawtow,[4] was a paratrooper with the Royal Lao Army. The first time he bought a bowl of noodles from her stand, Khamkong was so busy that she paid no attention to him. It took a week for her to realize he was coming to her every day, sometimes twice a day. She noticed he was purchasing the same thing each time: a large bowl of noodles, spicy with extra broth. On the eighth day, she asked if he wanted to try something new. He said, "Yes. Today, I would like to have my bowl of noodles, spicy with extra broth. And I would like to eat it sitting alongside of you."

From what I have heard, my grandfather was a true charmer. Though he was only three years older than Khamkong, his army uniform and the fact that he was almost six feet tall (very tall for a Lao man) made her think he was much older. He loved to socialize and was the life of the party. Khamkong, only four feet, eight inches, kept more to herself and did not particularly like large social settings. They were exact opposites, yet they fell in love over spicy noodles and married a year later.

My grandfather had many military assignments throughout the country, and as transportation in Laos was (and is still) a challenge because of the mountains and rivers, he would be gone for months, sometimes even years, at a time. Eventually, the marriage suffered.

Word got back to Khamkong that her husband had fallen in love with another woman in a village where he was stationed. Although it was culturally accepted for Lao men to have more than one wife, my grandmother was heartbroken. In a show of strength, she refused to accept a "typical" Lao husband.

Khamkong became a single mother to my mother and allowed her husband to visit their daughter from time to time. They lived in different villages, many difficult miles apart. She kept her distance and kept her pain all to herself.

Pawtow stayed involved as much as possible in his daughter's life and wanted to continue his relationship with Khamkong. But her trust was broken, and she was too proud and hurt to ever accept a

---

[4] "Pawtow" is the Lao word for "grandfather."

marriage that required sharing her husband with another woman. When he came to visit with my mother, Khamkong would be courteous but never spent more than a few minutes in his presence. This went on for more than 15 years.

My mother was already married with one child when my grandmother received news of Pawtow's passing. During the ongoing civil war, resulting from the communist coup, my grandfather was captured. Highly-ranked military and government officials such as my grandfather were held for years in the re-education camps. My grandmother never received word whether he was dead or alive, until the day, more than three years later, one of his colleagues showed up at her door with the hard news.

Pawtow was among 16 men captured together. They were tortured and beaten, made to do chores and strenuous work, and forced to recite teachings of the new way of life under the communist regime. They were starved; some days, they were given only one boiled egg to split between the 16 men. After several years, the regime finally released the men who remained alive. They had to find their own way by foot. Only six survived the journey home; my grandfather was not one of them.

He never left the grounds of the re-education camp. Badly starved and stricken with illness, with barely enough energy to lift his body from the floor, he asked his friends to find his family members and tell them good-bye on his behalf. And he asked the man who showed up at my grandmother's doorstep to request her forgiveness.

Soon after receiving the news of his passing, my grandmother agreed to make the trek across the Mekong to escape with my family. My mother, sisters and I have inherited the same vulnerable strength that saw my grandmother through years of love and loss (strength that has helped me survive my own loves and numerous losses). Her combined strength and sensitivity enabled her to leave everything she knew behind and to stand beside a family that needed her, which she continues to do to this day, as an 83 year-old matriarch. The work of her hands, heart and soul (her *sunay*), ensured our survival during those hard early years. Bolstered by her love, we even began to thrive in the strange new world of America.

"Unselfish Love"

I look at you, and your eyes remind me
of the selfishness that lives inside me.
I am blinded – yet guided by unnatural light,
a dimmed light blanketed by your pain.
Your smile captures my soul.
My laughter cannot compare to your sincerity.

Here you are again,
running through my mind.
You live to become a part of everything;
I merely breathe the air surrounding me, noting nothing.
I touch your brittle hand and you feel me.

By understanding how you see the world,
I learn to feel again.
I observe your pain, watching your face
and find no trace of tears –
only my own fall and streak my cheeks.

I walk away to keep you from seeing.
As I turn around to wave good-bye,
you smile more beautifully than ever before.
I look at you and allow it to be
a reminder of your unselfish love.

PART II

How I Learned to Shine
My True Light

How My Sister and I
Ended Up with a New Hairstyle

There was a time when I didn't want to look the way I do and be who I am. As a child, I did not look like the others; I had almond-shaped eyes, straight black hair and a smaller frame than the other children. We lived in southern Maryland, just across the border of southeast D.C., in a very low-income neighborhood. You could probably call it the "ghettos." There were no other Asian kids in our elementary school, which made me and my sister easy targets for ridicule. Mina and I suffered humiliation and cruelty at the hands of our peers in school and, most notoriously, on the bus.

As many kids know, the school bus can often be a hotbed of shame and antagonism. The bus my sister and I rode to and from school every day was no exception. The other kids called us "chinks" and told us that we smelled like fish from "the boat." But our parents had cautioned us not to get into trouble, so we simply ignored their remarks. I tried to keep a stony face, but all sorts of emotions bombarded my spirit: the loneliness of being an insignificant outsider, unwanted and alone, and the anger at the injustice of it all.

Though many of the children joined in on the "fun," there were two boys who were expert bullies, and they usually sat behind me and Mina. One was a bit overweight and the other as slender as a stick. They were always the loudest kids on the bus, cracking jokes on everyone and even arguing with each other at times. One particular afternoon, my sister and I were their targets. They began pushing their knees into the back of our seat and kicking it in order to provoke some type of response. Mina, true to her quiet, introverted nature, remained calm and collected, but I was getting angrier with each kick. She could sense my anxiety and put her right hand on my left arm to calm me.

The kicking and name calling continued to get harder and louder, and eventually my sister lost her temper, leapt up and twisted around in the seat so that she towered over the boys. "Quit it, or I'm going to climb over this seat and punch you both in the face!" she yelled. Impressed by her courage and surprised to see the pure anger in her eyes, the kids fell silent.

Our bus driver must have witnessed the scene from her mirror. She was a large woman with mocha-colored skin and short, curly hair. She didn't smile much and had a mean look about her, perhaps a result of hauling noisy kids around every day. When the bus driver heard Mina yelling, she screamed at her to sit down and told everybody to be quiet. My heart was beating hard and fast, as if I was channeling my sister's energy and adrenaline. That was the first time I saw Mina lose her temper.

When she settled back into her seat, I looked at her, but she didn't want to look at me. She stared straight ahead with no expression on her face, and we were silent for the rest of the bumpy ride home.

As our bus stop approached, I reached down to get my backpack and heard uncontrollable giggling from the bullies behind us. I turned around, curious to see what was so funny, and found them wrapping strands of chewed gum gently around the locks of my sister's hair. She didn't even notice, because the ride was so bumpy and the two kids had been able to contain their laughter until then.

My face felt hot as anger started to boil up inside of me. I jumped into the aisle and slapped both of their hands away from her head, which alerted Mina to the situation. She grabbed her hair; she no longer looked angry, just sad and lost.

The bus came to a stop and the driver made her way to our seats. The bus driver didn't say anything to me or Mina, but for a brief moment, her face did not appear so mean. She actually looked somber and disappointed. She began scolding the two boys, but I could not pay attention to what was being said. I simply stared into Mina's eyes, but she turned away. I felt an overwhelming sense of sympathy, followed by deep anger, an anger I could not express in words. There were no tears streaming down her face. I was shedding them for her.

The next day, Mina got a new hairstyle; her long, dark, straight hair became a short bob. She looked like a little china doll. My parents did not make a big deal of it. Instead of getting angry or indignant about the way we had been treated, Mai said that she had wanted to trim our hair for a long time and this was just a sign to finally do so. She asked if I wanted a trim, too, and to show solidarity with Mina, I nodded.

We never talked about this experience again, but I got a great deal more from it than a new hairstyle. I learned that we choose how we react in emotionally-challenging situations. My parents knew that we were hurt by the teasing, and their casual reaction was not insensitivity to our feelings. Instead, they were teaching us that we were strong enough to deal with what happened and to move on, with grace. There was no point in dwelling on the gum and the lost hair. We liked our new look, because our parents told us how lovely we were. So, we moved on, knowing a little more about how to choose the high road, even when you are stuck on the bus.

***

Chameleon

By the time I reached middle school, I was tired of living inside my Asian body, so I figured out how to "disguise" myself. I cherished my heritage, but for a budding teenager, it was exhausting to wake up every day knowing somebody would remind me what I looked like and how weird and different I was because of it. While some of my classmates may have been curious about who I was and where I came from, they rarely attempted to engage in conversation. Many were just indifferent toward us – the Asian minority. There were about 10 of us in the school, but we did not have much to do with one another. We were all just trying to lay low and avoid attention. Indifference was bad enough, but most of the time, we were the target of pointed cruelty.

Unfortunately, my ethnicity wasn't the only thing that made me stand out or made me a target. I was often ridiculed for being the teacher's pet and called a "nerd" for getting straight A's. I wanted to be invisible, but my peers always found a way to call me out. They even gave me a nickname – "Ms. Goody-Two-Shoes." Even my siblings called me this quite often. I felt bad because I believed what they were saying. True to my nickname, I was a people pleaser. I constantly doubted my actions and worried how I appeared to the world. I learned to be a chameleon and made myself flexible to the energy of the people around me. I got very good at figuring out how to adapt in order to feel the most calm and at peace, and I behaved accordingly.

Being flexible in my demeanor and personality helped me blend in well with different groups. But what really made me stand out, what always gave me away as an outsider, was my physical appearance, which wasn't as easy to change. But I was up to the challenge. The summer I was 13 years old, I made the commitment to spend every weekend playing in my father's garden so I could get a tan. I thought that if I got tan enough, I would fit in with the black kids, who made up about 85 percent of our student body. My mother would tell me to put on sun block, but there was no way I was going to deter the sun from darkening me up! I lied to my mother all summer, and I felt no guilt, only determination to "become" black.

It was like a race, and I only had three months until September, when school would start again. I wanted to be ready for a new beginning and the experience of finally being accepted. The previous year, I had observed and taken notes on the trends my peers considered "in style." Large-hoop earrings and colorful shirts with floral patterns were the hottest rage. I was determined that all my research would enable me to transform myself in the fall.

On the morning of the first day of seventh grade, I snuck into my mother's jewelry box to borrow her hoop earrings. She and Paw had already left for work so she wouldn't miss them. I had the perfect shirt already picked out, one abundant with floral prints. Tragically, my younger sister, Lola, was taking too long with her turn in the bathroom, and I forgot to grab the curling iron before she went in. My hair needed to be curled into tiny little spirals just like the other girls wore theirs last year. My anxiety grew. The moment I heard the bathroom door crack open, I ran in, grabbed the iron and began the task of curling strands upon strands of my thick hair. I had to hurry or I was going to be late for the bus.

My well-meaning grandmother made the situation worse by insisting I come eat my breakfast. I told her my tummy was upset and I wasn't hungry, but the truth was, my hair was nowhere near done. She eventually lost her patience with me and came upstairs to tell me if I didn't go down and put something in my stomach, she was going to feed me herself. I quickly finished up, ate breakfast and barely made the bus. I was finally off to be greeted with open arms by my peers.

While I didn't quite get the rock-star reception I hoped for, I did make some friends that school year. For a while, I attributed the success of my budding friendships and the feeling of acceptance to my new look. And then, one autumn morning, I looked into the mirror and realized, with a surge of panic, that my tan was fading!

I became so fearful in that moment. What if my façade fell away and my new friends discovered that I was Asian again? I didn't want to go back to the world where no one liked me, where no one wanted to be my friend. I began to cry. Suddenly, Lola knocked at the bathroom door and yelled, "Hurry up! It's my turn to shower, and I'm going to be late for school!" Oh well, there was nothing I could do about it now but go to school and prepare to be snubbed.

But all my friends greeted me as usual. I was beyond relieved that they did not notice my skin becoming lighter as winter approached. In fact, as the year went on, they greeted me the same way every day, throughout all the seasons I knew them. Looking back, I think the confidence I gained from feeling like I looked like everyone else primed my inner beauty so that it radiated outwards to draw people into my own bold light. And all the while, I thought it was my darker skin that made me so appealing!

Once I started to focus on my relationships and who I was being, rather than my appearance, my anxiety began to fade away – little by little. Eventually, I no longer worried about the color of my skin determining whether my friends wanted to be a part of my life. My tears did not again flow over a faded tan … until college.

"Move"

They say she moves truly like no other
Clothed in judgment; wrapped with heavy hope
Dodged a few bright corners
Afraid to see beyond their scope.

Sat alongside the night through so many moons
Waited for shelter to show up too soon
Many hearts swayed like branches of willow trees
Only the strong can withstand her past pains, those eccentricities.

She really does move like so many others
One slight step forward, each foot in front of the other.

All Work and No Play

My parents depended on me and Mina for support – cultural and financial – even as children. The language barrier made it hard for them to communicate with the outside world and handle the day-to-day business of maintaining a household. So, we took on the main responsibilities of translating and helping to make financial and business decisions for our family. I have a vivid memory of being nine years old, opening an envelope and reading a bill to my father. To this day, I read all the official documents that come for my mother and grandmother.

As Mina and I got older, we took on even more responsibility – helping to pay some of the bills we translated for our parents. At age 15, as soon as I could get a work permit, I found a job at a Taco Bell. Mina worked at a local convenience store called Dash-In. We contributed half of our income to family household needs. The rest we saved for college, understanding that our parents were not in a position to help us with tuition. Mina and I always knew that college was a necessity, not a luxury. We wanted a way out of financial hardship and to be able to help our family financially. That meant college. I already had my future as a college graduate planned out in my mind and was committed to doing whatever I could to ensure my dream would come true – from earning money to participating in extracurricular activities.

Mina and I had our routine down. She was old enough to drive, and Paw bought her a white Toyota Corolla for transportation to and from work after school. Our schedule was choreographed with precision to ensure we could fit in school and work, as well as extracurricular activities. Mina drove us to school early in the morning so I could tutor students struggling in math for an hour before the first class began. The normal school day ended at 2:30 p.m. After school on Mondays and Wednesdays, we participated in the aesthetics club, a group that fed my creative soul – a side of me that barely had an opportunity to come out and play. By my second year in high school, I made it into the National Honor Society, which met once a week after school. I also signed up to be a statistician for our boy's soccer team. All these activities held their own pleasures, but I also hoped to show my character strengths and community engagement on college scholarship applications.

By 5:00 p.m., Mina and I would be on our way to work. My shift began at 6:00, and she picked me up after she got off at 11:30. When we finally got home around midnight, our studies and homework would be waiting for us. We usually crawled in bed by 1:30 or 2:00 in the morning, setting our alarms for 5:00 a.m. in order to begin again. The cycle continued throughout high school.

My parents often worried about our work load. My father, a sensitive man, felt guilty that he was not in a better position to provide us with the freedom and flexibility most of our peers enjoyed. Many of my friends at school did not have to work; if they did, it was for extra spending money. It was hard for them to comprehend my schedule, and sometimes they gave me a hard time for not being able to hang out with them more. I often wished I could go to parties and sleepovers with my girlfriends. I couldn't even take my dating life seriously.

I was so focused on saving money, studying hard and going to college to re-design my path (and the future of my family) that I neglected to offer my full attention and heart to anything but my books and my work.

I had romantic interests here and there, but in all of those cases, I was more their girlfriend than they were my boyfriends. I didn't open my heart up much to anyone because I didn't want to hurt anyone; my focus was not on romance, it was on survival. Looking back, I realize that my laser-sharp focus on a more stable future, as well as all the pressure I placed on myself, broke a few hearts along the way – including mine. But I could not see or feel much pain because I was exhausted all the time.

"A Lesson from a Homeless Stranger"

I watch you stand in the rain
and the chilling air, a blanket
covers your body to protect
from the sting, to protect
what little is left of your spirit.

The heaviness of these clouds
covers all purifying light.
I want to go beyond the ache
of seeing your loneliness and feel,
for the moment, your helplessness.

Pretense: a body of materialistic minds
covers me, shapes me into someone
who pities you.

For a moment, I stand where you stand
under your blanket, under
these heavy clouds, helpless
and as alone.
You do not pretend as I do.
I feel, at times, as lonely as you.

Crush(ed)

My heart was aflutter. It was my sophomore year at the University of Maryland, and I had developed a major crush on a boy – one who was tall with light-brown hair and brilliant, blue eyes. I had never spoken with him but I felt a taste of what I thought must be love – something sweet and tangy. Little did I know how bittersweet this kind of infatuation can be. Of course, no one could have enlightened me at the time; I was like one of those cartoon characters with heart-shaped eyes.

I first spotted Mr. Blue Eyes at McKeldin Library in the fall semester. Still as studious as I was in elementary school, I spent a lot of time there. He got off the elevator on the second floor, where all the study tables and cubicles were, as I got on. He caught my attention when he looked into my eyes and smiled. I thought to myself, "Wow, what kind eyes."

That semester, I studied on the second floor of McKeldin on Mondays and Wednesdays. He must have had the same break between classes because he was usually there. While trying to study, I observed him covertly. With his nose to the books, rarely looking up to take a break, he was as studious as me (at least when I wasn't distracted by cute boys with dreamy eyes).

I imagined him to be a gentle soul. His demeanor was soft and subtle. The energy around him always felt calm, even in the way he placed his jacket on his seat, gently pulled out his books and neatly organized them on the desk. Yet, there was also a clumsiness and awkwardness (even a shyness) about him when he interacted with others. I could picture us being great study partners and friends. I imagined he would calm my raging energy and help me stay still for more than 10 minutes. I saw him as a Clark Kent type and often fantasized about who he might be outside of the library. Perhaps I was hoping for Superman. This will sound funny to those who know me well, but at that time in my life, I truly wanted someone to whisk me away and save me from my hectic life.

I pined for Mr. Blue Eyes for two full years, continuing to silently observe him in the library. I never made a move to speak with this beautiful portrait of a man. I didn't even know his name.

He often made eye contact with me and almost always smiled in acknowledgement. I would awkwardly grin and quickly shift my eyes back down to my books. But I thought his smiles must mean that he was at least somewhat interested.

The crush continued to grow, and before I knew it, the end of my junior year was fast approaching. A panicked thought occurred to me: what if this was his senior year? If I didn't express my feelings before graduation day, would I have a missed opportunity on my hands?

I finally shared my crush with Rafael, my best friend since an intense Spanish literature class during our sophomore year. Rafael, an outgoing and vivacious person, could not believe I had let two years go by without even a "hello" to my handsome mystery man. He was so frustrated with my risk aversion that he threatened to share my feelings with Mr. Blue Eyes if I didn't talk to him before the last week of the semester. I told him to just let it be. Nothing was going to come of it. I knew nothing about this guy.

One week before finals, Rafael and I sat on the third floor of the library, which gave us a great view of the second floor study area. Mr. Blue Eyes was there. I took a break from my studies and said to Rafael, "I wonder what will happen to him in life after college."

Rafael stared at me, took a deep breath and said, "Mali, I have had enough! No more wondering. Why don't you just ask him yourself? If you don't, I will gladly go down there and do it for you!" I started laughing, sure that he was joking as usual. But he was not laughing, and almost as if in slow motion, he pushed his chair away from his desk, got up and walked away.

I called out to him in as firm a voice as I dared to use in the library the week before finals. But Rafael did not look back. The next few minutes felt unbearable. I was paralyzed. I wanted to get up and stop him, but my feet would not budge; only my heart moved – at its maximum rate. I could only observe from above as Rafael gracefully glided through the second floor study area, tapped Mr. Blue Eyes on the shoulder, knelt down on one knee and spoke to him. The silence on the third floor was deafening. I buried my head inside my arms. All I could do was wait for his return.

When Rafael came back a few minutes later to recount the story, he found me red with anger and mortification. I could barely swallow and my face began to burn as Rafael recounted his story. It went something like this:

"Excuse me," said Rafael. "I'm sorry to bother you, but do you know my friend, the Asian girl I'm always here studying with?"

My crush nodded and presented Rafael with that smile I had come to appreciate so much. Rafael told him about my interest in knowing him better and asked what he thought about it.

"She seems very nice and is pretty," said Mr. Blue Eyes. "But the truth is, I am simply not attracted to Asians."

That was all Rafael told me. Understanding my sensitivity to such a topic, he waited for me to take it in.

All of the sudden, my little girl, the one who was so adamant about tanning every summer, resurfaced. Now, I wished my hair was blond and that I had brilliant, blue eyes to match his. Perhaps if my eyes were less almond-shaped, he would have been the one to show up in front of me instead of Rafael. Perhaps then, there would be a totally different version of this story. But the reality of the situation made all my fantasies clatter to the ground. I felt like the entire library could hear my heart shattering.

Tears rolled down my face, and Rafael offered me his hand. "Mali, he only feels that way because that's all he has to go by," he said. "If he spent time getting to know who you are and not just what you look like, he would love you like I do."

Deep down, I knew that he was right, but at the time, all I could see was the invisible mirror that popped up in front of my face to remind me once again what my outer core looked like and that somehow others did not see its beauty.

I instantly regressed from a 21-year-old woman to a 13-year-old girl. I was transported to my seventh grade classroom, where I sat next to my child-model friend, Lauri, with her long, curly, blond hair and blue eyes. Steven, with his sandy-blond hair and light-brown eyes, walked toward our seats, and my heart began to race. I had developed a major crush on this classmate of mine. I thought about him every morning on the bus ride to school and fantasized about him offering to carry my backpack and walk to me to my next class.

Steven had approached me in class several times with questions about homework, and in my mind, I made that mean he was flirting with me. As he walked toward us, I expected him to grab the seat next to me and at least ask me another homework question. Instead, he smiled at Lauri and walked right by me as though I was invisible. He sat directly behind her and said, "The color of your eyes is so nice, and I really think you're pretty today." She responded with a loud giggle. I looked at him and smiled. He pretended like he didn't know me and walked away. Lauri looked over to see my reaction, but I wasn't sure what to do. I wanted to shrivel up and hide (or steal Lauri's body).

I left McKeldin library that day, nine years later, feeling the same way I felt when I slunk out of my seventh grade classroom – heartbroken. Disappointed in the man I once thought was so full of beauty and kindness, inside and out, I didn't go back to the second floor for the rest of the semester.

Now, I can look back on that experience and realize that I was no different than him. I made certain assumptions about Mr. Blue Eyes and based all of my emotions and expectations on his outer core. I never considered who he was and what his preferences were. I never even learned his name. I understand now how fantasies put up a glass wall around reality and that those walls shatter eventually. All is forgiven.

***

"Innocence"

Oh, how I wish to be innocent as a child,
to laugh and play,
to cry and not have to explain my tears . . .

I'd like to dream of clear blue skies
and bright moonlit nights,
a touch of sun, a sprinkle of rain . . .

Once upon a time, I could do this,
before I knew what nightmares were.

But now, I see no perfect blue sky to hope upon,
no chance to stop the pain in the world,
no curing a disease with love.
My hands bleed and sting from trying to clear a path
through this dark wood, back to childhood.

No one keeps promises anymore.
With piles of torn letters and boxes full of old photos,
I am left shattered.

Oh, how I wish to be like you, child.
You wipe my tears and promise a better day tomorrow.
Oh, naivety . . . mine or yours?

Returning Home with Two Suitcases and the Beginnings of Self Love

At a local supermarket in Madrid, Spain, my host mother Eva turned to me and said, "*Si vas a tener exito en tus estudios internacional, no puedes hablar en Ingles conmigo. Hoy, voy a ensenarte como ir de compras en Espana.*"[5] She was explaining to me that because I'd taken eight years of Spanish and come on this trip to improve my skill with her native language, she was forbidding me to speak English with her.

I was 20 years old, and studying abroad in Spain was scary enough, but staying with a host mother who did not allow English in her household was beyond intimidating. Having only spoken the language in a classroom setting, conversational Spanish was no small challenge. But Eva declared that she was determined for me to do well with my studies. Today, she would teach me how to go to the grocery store for all our necessities. Then, I would be expected to do it alone.

As we walked into that grocery store three days after I arrived in Spain, she wanted me to do my best to speak with the butchers and bakers in Spanish. I had never seen such things as *prosciutto, serrano ham and lomo cabeza,* and I had no idea how to properly ask for the right amount, cut and size. Eva laughed when she saw the little-girl expression on my face that said, "Please don't make me go to the grocery store by myself ever. I can't do this without you." So, she guided me to the counter and announced to the young, handsome Spaniard behind the register that I was staying with her for the next three months as an international student.

She requested that he take good care of me and help me buy groceries, as doing so would be my weekly homework assignment. He laughed, winked at me and said not to worry; the shop owners and staff would take good care of me throughout my stay. I felt much better after that.

---

[5] Translation: "If you are going to be successful with your international studies, you cannot speak English with me. Today, I am going to teach you how to shop in Spain."

Eva gave me a tour of the store, pointing out all the different produce items that were popular in Madrid and the various types of meats and seafood dishes. This was the first time I saw blood sausages and octopus cooked with its own ink. I loved seeing jars upon jars of *sangria*, inhaling the smell of fresh bread and counting the bottles of extra virgin Spanish olive oil lined up along the windowsill of the shop.

When we arrived at the register with our grocery items, I noticed four young men standing behind the counter. I recognized the handsome clerk who had promised to take care of me. The other gentlemen stood behind him, smiling and greeting me with, *"Hola, senorita! Buenos dias!"*[6]

Eva began to giggle and said something I didn't understand at the time. I thought it was Spanish slang but later discovered that it was normal conversation; I still had not adjusted to the Madrileno dialect.

The men all spoke up at the same time with laughter and smiles – all looking directly at me. I was getting uncomfortable and embarrassed, fearing they were mocking me. Eva noticed that I did not understand their dialogue. After a few more words with them, she asked to pay for our items, and we were on our way back home.

On our walk, I turned to her, and careful to speak in my best Spanish, asked her to translate what the men had said into English. She explained with a giggle, "I told them to behave when I send you there for groceries. They told me they couldn't keep such a promise, because you are so beautiful and it is a treat for them to see a young, beautiful Asian woman visiting from the United States. They asked about your ethnic background and if you were American born. When I told them you were from Laos, they were all intrigued, because you are the first Lao person they ever met."

[6] Translation: "Hello, miss! Good day!"

Four days later, I was back at the shop, with my little Spanish-English dictionary in my purse just in case. When I walked through the door, Jorge, my young, handsome friend, greeted me with his wink. *"Hola, Senorita Mali,"* he said with a conspiratorial smile, which meant he was going to take good care of me and it would be our little secret from my host mother. I was truly impressed that he remembered my name. Within 30 minutes, I was ready to check out with my bottle of wine, fresh bread, a pound of serrano ham and eggs. Of course, Jorge helped by taking the shopping list Eva wrote out for me and doing all my shopping, which he did every time I came in the store afterward.

While he shopped, he asked questions about Laos and how I came to live in America. In my broken Spanish (and with some help from my dictionary), I made my best attempt to tell the story. When I didn't understand his questions, he continued to smile forgivingly. In fact, after a short while, he told me that he was truly impressed with my Spanish. With my confidence lifted, I placed my dictionary back inside my purse. I stopped thinking in English to find the right context before translating in my head to Spanish. It was with Jorge's help that I spent the rest of my time in Spain speaking from the heart. My Spanish flowed, and I learned as I went along.

It was also because of Jorge and his handsome friends at the shop that I truly began to appreciate my own "beauty" as a Lao-American woman. Every time I went grocery shopping, I felt like a goddess. The men and women working there glowed with excitement as they greeted me with two kisses upon my cheek and hearts full of interest and warmth. Bella became my nickname. It means "beautiful lady."

Over time, my Spanish became less broken, and I started to take on the Madrilenos accent. I ended almost every sentence with *"vale, vale,"* which is how the younger folks spoke to one another. It means, "OK, OK," which seemed appropriate, because everything in Spain for me felt *"vale, vale."*

One afternoon, on my way home from school, I decided to stop
by the shop for milk before siesta time hit, when the shops closed
for the afternoon. Jesus, one of the shop keepers, was there closing
up. He invited me and my other exchange-student friends for an
insider's tour of the night life in Madrid – with him and his friends
as our guides.

Night life in Madrid starts really late. That evening, I met four
of my classmates at the Plaza de Mayor at 11:00 p.m. for dinner.
Afterwards, Jesus, Jorge and two of their other friends met us at one
of the popular dance clubs. The guys had strong connections with
the club manager, so as soon as we got to the line, the bouncers
waved to Jesus and directed us to go to the second floor. I was not
yet legal to drink in the United States, but those rules did not apply
in Spain. No one checked my ID, and Jorge immediately went off
to order me a glass of *sangria*.

Suddenly, I had three guys, all strangers, standing around me and
asking if I needed anything from the bar. It felt like they were
competing for my attention, and I didn't know who to answer or
acknowledge first. They all assumed I spoke Spanish and continued
to speak to me with ease – which was quite fascinating to me. I told
them I would ask my friends to join me, but they weren't interested
in hanging out with my friends.

I turned around to look for my girlfriends. I spotted them standing
together on the dance floor, waving at me. Nobody was talking to
them. I was shocked. My girlfriends were beautiful. Two had blond
hair and blue eyes. One was a beautiful red-head with cute freckles.
And there I was, the Asian girl who was called an "ugly duckling" in
elementary and middle school. What was this world I had stepped
into, where looking Asian was a source of intrigue and beauty?

Jorge turned around with our drinks in his hands. I caught his
eye and sent a silent message for him to "rescue" me – ASAP. He
laughed from afar and winked his usual wink, helping me feel safe
as he made his way toward us. "*Hombres, por favor, ella es mi novia
de Laos,*" he said to the men, telling me I was his girlfriend from
Laos.[7] Still, they did not budge. In fact, they became even more

---

[7] Translation: "Guys, please, this is my girlfriend from Laos."

fascinated and started telling Jorge how lucky he was to find such a beautiful Asian girlfriend. They asked how we met. Jorge told them he owned a grocery shop, and the moment I entered his store for the first time with my host mother, he fell for me.
I laughed, but for the rest of my stay in Spain, he was so attentive and lovely to me that I wondered later if he might have been telling the truth about the way he felt for me.

I was so alive that night. I didn't dance much but I spent the rest of the night introducing my friends to our new friends. Out of my classmates, I had spent the most time studying Spanish, so I bounced from one friend to the next – the liaison, translator and matchmaker for the night.

Jorge and Jesus had a heck of a time controlling all the different men who wanted to dance with my classmates. Spanish men can be quite persistent after a few cervezas and some hard liquor. Fortunately, I was with my "boyfriend," Jorge, but that did very little to deter some men from grabbing my waist and pulling me to dance with them. Each person with whom I came into contact at the club, including the women, wanted to know about me and my origins. In fact, everyone I met throughout my stay in Spain was fascinated by my outer core and wanted to learn more about the person behind the image. I had never experienced anything like that in the United States I had never felt so beautiful and free to fully share my identity, my story and my ethnicity the way the Spaniards compelled me to do. The more I shared about my inner person with this appreciative audience, the more I began to fall in love with my outer self.

On the night of our graduation from the summer program, the instructor took us all out for dinner to celebrate. I'm not sure how we came to choose an upscale Chinese restaurant, but we all met there at 10:00 p.m. I remember tasting the chicken with broccoli dish and thinking, "Chinese food in Spain tastes so different than in the United States." Not better or worse, just different. My classmates were all speaking in Spanish with more ease and confidence than ever. The conversation around the table was lively and bright.

A petite waitress came to take our dessert order. She spoke broken Spanish with a thick Chinese accent. I was fascinated by her. After she walked away, I turned to my instructor and said in Spanish, "It's just so strange to see an Asian woman speaking Spanish." He gave me a very puzzled look. I was perplexed, and as he began howling with laughter, the humor of my comment dawned on me. He told me to excuse myself from the table and go find a mirror.

For the first time in my life, I had forgotten that I was Asian. It just didn't matter as it had always mattered before. I began to laugh hysterically at myself, in celebration. I still saw color all around me but I did not allow it to define me anymore. To this day, I cherish the beautiful epiphany I had at that Chinese restaurant.

Spain fell in love with *all* of me. She was curious and interested, and always made me feel safe to open up and be whoever I wanted to be. She helped me *want* to be me. At the end of the summer, I waved a sweet farewell with gratitude in my heart. I returned home in late August with two suitcases and the beginnings of self love.

"Southern Spain"

Patterns on crusted ceramic
The ancient gods knew how to finger paint
Mountains peaked while towns hid
Rocks were pushed along by the currents
drifting from place to place
Orange trees lined the cobblestone streets
Alleyways of beggars and pleaders roamed beneath balconies
Eyes filled the air with curiosity, hearts afraid to reach out
afraid to ask too much
The sea brushed against tired feet,
cleansing, caressing, leaving and allowing peaceful breath to escape closed lips
Hush; the gardens sang with subtlety
The tide loosed her hold, letting life pull toward the shores.

✷✷✷

The Gravitational Pull of Good Listening

While I did not have much time or energy for friends and boyfriends in my youth, my relationships with my brother and sisters have always been strong and rich. I continue to nurture distinct and unique relationships with each of my siblings. They spoke to me in confidence about their deepest concerns, and I am honored to be the one they trust. When we were little, time and time again, one of my siblings would come to me and say, "Please don't tell anyone else about this. I trust only you and need your support and advice." For whatever reason, the gravitational pull of trust resonated from within me, and those around me found themselves sharing things they would otherwise be afraid to utter out loud.

It was also like this with my parents. Sometimes my father and mother, as well as my grandmother, would share stories with me, events they had never spoken of before, often surprising themselves that such stories had escaped their lips.

Listening is easy for me. When people come to me and begin to reveal themselves, it's almost like a switch cuts off the clattering of my own thoughts. I can push aside all the noise and allow others to safely release the chaos in *their* minds. This, believe it or not, is like a refuge from my own negativity. Sometimes, because of my worries and fears, I am not able to be as present and available as someone needs me to be, but it is my nature to be honest and diplomatic, to offer to call the next day when space opens up in my world so that I can genuinely show up and truly listen. Allowing others to share beautiful and painful thoughts brings me back into balance because it reminds me that I am not alone. We all have fears and anxieties. While I am still learning to freely share my own, I have the ability to be an intent listener.

My grandmother believes I have a gift. I often find it easy to connect with people from the moment I meet them and I enjoy creating space for the authenticity of each new encounter. I show up without boundaries or barriers, without hard-and-set expectations from each new relationship. Life somehow feels more light and interesting this way. Grandma says that certain people have this "little something special" about them, and you can pick them out by watching how children and animals gravitate toward them.

I never knew of such gifts. I took these types of things for granted. But I have come to believe that there is magic and energy in the design of our natural inner cores. We are all unique; we possess special traits and abilities, but most of us don't understand how valuable they are and how much our abilities can impact the people our lives touch. Most of us are not conditioned to celebrate our special qualities; we have been trained by our environment and society to seek and work on finding our better selves "somewhere out there." But wherever you go, there you are. It's difficult for all of us, I think, to remember that we have everything we need already inside of us. It's just a matter of valuing our gifts and deciding how to use them.

Like the elephant, who can feel empathy when most other animals cannot, it begins with self-awareness. First, we recognize our own faces in the mirror. Then, we look inward and discover the value and strength there, which enables us to be a calming presence and support for others. In a miraculous transformation, we become fireflies, whose light guides others.

As I get older, I keep my eyes and ears open for proof of my grandmother's theory about my own unique ability. I see it with my two nephews sometimes. When they are in a crowded room, they run around like typical little boys. But when they have alone time with Auntie, they naturally share with me.

My older nephew, Hunter, is much more introverted than his younger brother, Jaden. He spends a lot of time in his room, playing on his computer or building with his Lego set. I often go into his room, ask to sit on his bed and do some work while he "works." He will smile and nod, and after a few minutes of silence, he will begin to share.

One afternoon when he was seven years old, as we were hanging out in his room, busy at our work, Hunter said, "Auntie, did you know that most dinosaurs had feathers, but many of them could not fly because their bones were too heavy?"

"Wow. I didn't know that," I replied. "That's pretty cool."

He looked up at me from his Lego set. "Yeah, it's pretty cool that they had feathers, but it makes me sad that their heaviness kept them from flying. It makes me sad that I don't have feathers and can't fly." His eyes dropped, and he went back to building.

I looked over and saw that in his hand were pieces that resembled a helicopter in the making. I couldn't help but smile. "Well, sweetie," I said, "you may not have been born with feathers but you can certainly build your own wings and see the world someday. You're about to put all the pieces together and build that helicopter sitting in your hands right now. If you really want to, you will find a way to fly."

He lifted the helicopter from his palms and said, "Yeah, just a couple more pieces, and I'll be ready to fly. Can you help me find the missing pieces, Auntie?"

He and I worked silently on our separate projects for about an hour that afternoon. Every time he completed the building of a new object, he would bring it to me for inspection. I would kiss his forehead and say, "Excellent job!" and in gratitude, he would kiss my nose. In his excitement, his kisses were often fast ones, usually missing my cheeks because I didn't turn fast enough for him.

I remember and reflect on this five-minute conversation with my nephew whenever I'm faced with daunting tasks or living inside moments where I fear the impossibilities of life. I'm glad I was there, present and attentive, in order to receive the lesson. So, if I do have a special gift that compels people to share their dreams and stories with me, it is a gift that continually blesses me as long as I use it.

"Shine"

Painful tears used to flow here,
down the cracks of these laugh lines
(You were the one
I used to run to).
Together, our smiles created moon shine,
the natural kind.

Broken was how I used to feel,
a victim of life lessons thrown at me too soon
a little girl lost, then.
Now, I stand before you: a woman
dancing and singing her own tune

Fallen, I crawled to find safe ground.
These days, I rise
beyond the tops of mountains
toward unknown skies.
Like a window without curtains, my heart is wide open;
I am alive.

Joyful tears now accompany those laugh lines.
One step after the other;
it was simply a matter of time.
This is a new place,
a lovely, peaceful space
Here I am,
making a choice to shine.

PART III

THE HEART-WRENCHING
TENSION OF LOVE
AND LOSS

Christopher – an Invocation

Your presence keeps me hanging on.
Your spirit fuels my strength to continue forward.
I am stronger than I ever knew;
I am wiser and more at peace because of you.

While my world feels as though it is standing still,
the universe flows ever more.
Like a river, my heart twists, bends and churns.
My mind wants simply to find rest.

I now hold conversations with the moon and butterflies.
The moon responds by shifting the stars,
and butterflies gently touch my forehead.
The fall breeze greets me every morning; winter's freshness draws near.

Your face I can no longer touch,
yet your soft voice I will forever hear.
I miss my gentle soul mate.
I want to kiss your protective hands.

And although the world looks different now,
there was never a need to say our final good-bye.
I feel you with me in every way;
I hear your laughter inside the sun with each new day.

Romance and Delight

I met Chris in July of 1998, and that deep green month will always fill me with emotion.

After a blissful two and a half weeks in sunny Spain, (my second trip there, this time with my godmother and sister as a graduation present), I began my first job as a college graduate. I found a position with a high-tech company named Unitech, which was looking to expand its market reach for computer-based training and to take the company to international markets within three to five years. My degrees in Marketing, Spanish and International Business, as well as my ability to speak multiple languages, made me a good fit.

I was so excited to begin this new phase of my life. The first day of work, I was filled with anxiety and butterflies fluttered in my stomach. Ellen, one of the project managers, welcomed me with a smile and led me on a tour. Our first stop was my new desk.

Upon entering what would be my cubicle, I heard some shuffling of paper and the sound of rolling wheels. This didn't prevent my surprise when a handsome man, seated on a rolling office chair, came flying out from behind the cubicle connected to mine. He halted his chair just before it began to spin him around, jumped up, and with his right hand positioned on his hip, extended his left hand to greet me with a sturdy handshake. Rolling chairs aside, this was an interesting way to greet someone. Most people extend their right hand to greet others. At five feet, 11 inches, he had a slender yet very athletic build, light-brown hair, and beautiful, blue eyes. There was warmth in his smile, and he had a gentle, tender way of carrying himself. I knew at that point that this man was different, even special.

"So great to meet ya!" he said. "I've heard a lot about my new office mate and I think we are going to have a wonderful time learning and sharing. I'm excited to have you on board. Welcome." He spoke so fast and his energy was so infectious that all I could do was grin from ear to ear and extend my hand awkwardly, not knowing how to receive a left-handed shake. He acted clumsily sweet. I giggled and thanked him for his excitement.

Christopher Meehan, my new office mate, was a marketing representative who'd been there almost a year. He was assigned to be my mentor and to teach me about the company's products and services. As one of the first commercial marketing representatives hired, my job was to learn as much as possible so I could help transition these products into commercial markets. Later that evening, I wrote in my journal: "I met Chris, my mentor. I think he is going to change my life." No words have ever been more true.

I was 22 years old when we met, and he was 28. At the time, I was living with my family in Maryland to save money. Each morning, I drove over the Woodrow Wilson Bridge to get from Upper Marlboro, Maryland, to Fairfax, Virginia. Traffic in the D.C. area is no fun. Some days it took me two hours to get to work – and two-and-a-half hours to get home. Occasionally, I would find myself nodding off behind the wheel, so I learned how to keep my mind occupied through positive thoughts and daily affirmations. Some days, I listened to inspiring music (and sang along at the top of my lungs). My daydreams were usually filled with romantic ideals, like finding a nice, quality guy to spend time with. I was in a much better place in life now that I was past those long hours of working at the fast-food restaurant and studying until 2:00 a.m. I felt more rested and had room for the things I enjoyed such as writing, dancing and singing – and for romance. Those long commutes home were physically exhausting but they also allowed me a "quiet" space to process and dream.

My commutes *to* work were a different story. I was more irritated, because really, I just wanted to get to work. Traffic was horrendous from Maryland to Virginia; cars would crawl along at 10 miles-an-hour for 10 to 15 miles. I'd often have to slap myself to keep from falling asleep behind the wheel. I commuted for five months, and Chris would always be the first one to hear my complaints. Every morning, I began our day together with the same litany: "I hate traffic. I have no social life because I spend five hours a day in my car. I'm exhausted and irritated before I even get here to start my full day!"

Chris indulged me. We began to develop a routine. He would get to the office first and wait to start our meeting with a cup of coffee. Within two weeks of knowing me, he knew how I liked it (light and sweet) and would have a hot cup waiting for me. Eventually, he also started leaving multivitamins alongside the coffee cup – maybe because he was sick of hearing my constant complaints about being tired from the ride.

He thought of my coffee and vitamins every day for the entire two years we worked together at Unitech. He thought of me even after they moved us into offices of our own on opposite ends of the building. He remained my mentor in many areas of my life beyond our working relationship.

Starting that day in July when he came wheeling around the corner into my life, my love for Chris grew subtly and naturally. I didn't even realize I was falling in love with him until after I was already there.

Trust in Me

Beloved, you did not expect me to show up here
with my left-handed greeting,
endless cups of coffee made special for you,
and my whole-hearted care,
becoming part of your life.
Maybe fate has forced us together.
Perhaps your heart is setting you free
to love me.

To love as you have never loved before.

The world is foggy.
Beloved, you search for a reason,
some sign of light.
I symbolize hope for brighter days;
reach out and take hold of me.

I want to stay like this forever.
Won't you trust in love again?

Trust in me.

Asian Fetish

After almost two months of working together, Chris offered to get me a month-long guest pass to his gym. "This way," he explained, "instead of leaving here at 5:30 every night only to sit in traffic for two hours, you can go work out, focus on your health, and then get home in 40 minutes, arriving at the same time you would anyway. What do you think?"

I lit up, "I think you are brilliant, Chris." That evening, he gave me a tour of the gym, showed me how to use all the machines and set me free. We agreed to meet outside of the locker room area, where there was a lounge and a view of the tennis courts below. We sat there and talked until 8:30 p.m. When I realized how late it was, I excused myself to call home and have my parents start dinner without me.

He invited me to check out his townhouse and meet his two roommates, Matt and Colby. At first, I was hesitant. This would be crossing a line from co-workers to personal friends. While I enjoyed being around Chris, the boundaries of our relationship had been formed along the clear and comfortable context of our work and his mentorship. He sensed my hesitation and pulled back. "We'll hang out with my roommates and order food and then you can head home," he said. "That way, I will feel better that you have eaten dinner ... but only if you are comfortable." It was hard to argue with that logic, so I accepted his invitation.

After dinner, while Matt and Colby played video games, Chris gave me a tour of the house. When we got to his bedroom, I looked around at the décor and found myself surrounded by Asian-inspired items. I felt a little uncomfortable, thinking for a split second that perhaps he had an Asian fetish or something. I began to laugh out loud.

"What's so funny?" he asked.

"Nothing!" I responded quickly through my laughter.

"What?"

I couldn't control myself. "Uh, Chris," I said. "Look around! Asian swords, wall tapestries of Japanese art, books about Taoism, Ying and Yang symbols, and awards for all your Tai Chi and Martial Arts achievements? I'm almost afraid that you have an Asian fetish!"

He looked around with fresh eyes. "Oh my God," he exclaimed, now laughing uncontrollably with me. "You are right! Except for the Asian fetish part though! I've never even dated an Asian woman before!"

Once we settled down, and I wiped the tears away from exercising my funny bone, he explained that he became interested in Asian arts and philosophies as a young boy, beginning with martial arts. His father, a one-star brigadier general, had traveled the globe and exposed his wife and children to other cultures. Chris knew more about other countries and cultures than I did at that time. His family moved around every few years when he was growing up, so he easily made friends with all kinds of people. As he shared more, I came to understand that he was able to make friends but found it difficult to keep them. Chris said he didn't allow too many people to get close because he knew that eventually, he would have to move away. This explained a lot. Many people loved being around Chris's infectiously positive energy, but he could count on one hand the people he actually considered true friends.

He shared much of his personal life with me that night. He even felt safe enough to tell me that he was still heartbroken from losing his mother two years prior to cancer. I could have listened to him, receiving and creating sacred space for his memories, for hours.

This side of Chris was not that different from the Chris I had become accustomed to at work, where he was just as transparent and curious to learn my thoughts and opinions. We spent another two hours, sitting on the edge of his bed, chatting it up. Around midnight, he walked me to my car and thanked me for making the time for us to get to know each other outside of work.

He was brave that night. He was always brave actually. He hugged me, and as if there was no need to worry about consequences, gently kissed me goodnight. It was that easy.

I smiled in return. He winked and held my car door open for me. "Drive home safe and call me when you get there, OK?"

"I will," I replied. "See you in the morning."

The next morning and all the mornings over the next five years, we continued to grow in our friendship and love. It was surreal how at ease my heart, body, mind and spirit felt during my entire relationship with Chris. Those who knew us as a couple will tell you that this is not an overstatement. We were the picture of steady and healthy love.

I learned so much about patience, acceptance, compromise and unconditional support from my five years with him. Like the monk who carries a warm, glowing coal beneath his robe through the winter months, I carry those lessons with me now in each present moment. They burn sometimes, but they also light my path and warm my soul.

How Love Taught Me to Fly

One afternoon at work, Chris stopped by my office. It was a quiet day, and we were bored. I don't remember what we were joking about, but soon we were howling with laughter. Though he was usually very serious and professional at work, he also had an amazing sense of humor. Chris's laugh, a girlish giggle, was remarkable, and he could make me laugh until it hurt to breathe. Hearing his giggle is what kept me laughing even when the joke was no longer that funny.

We got in trouble with our supervisor that afternoon. She yelled at us for causing so much commotion, but by the end of her scolding, we got her giggling like a little girl too. She left the office mumbling, "You two are impossible. You're so alike!"

He looked over at me. "You think we are alike? You know, we should try something! Why don't you write down the top 20 things you want to do before you die. Let's compare how alike we are by the end of this game."

I took the challenge. After 15 minutes, we exchanged lists. He started to call mine out and asked me to circle all the ones on his list that were the same.

"Skydiving," he read from my list.

"Got it," I said, circling the word on his list.

"Climbing Mt. Everest."

"A backpacking trip through the Swiss Alps," I read.

"Australian adventure!"

"We match," I exclaimed.

It was so bizarre. Chris and I had more than 12 matching dreams. That surprised us, and we sat there helping each other take a second look. "Oh my goodness, Chris," I said, "This is freaking me out!"

"Don't be freaked out! Let's start with the first thing on your list that is also on mine and plan to go do it together."

One month later, in mid-October, Chris and I drove out with some co-workers to Orange County, Virginia, for our first adventure together – skydiving! That first skydiving experience was beyond liberating.

As we fell 13,000 feet, my tandem instructor yelled, "We are falling through an ice cloud. If you get nauseated and feel like you're going to faint, hold your head up higher and take in deep, slow breaths!" I held my head high and took in those slow, deep breaths as the wind continued to punch me in the face. After a few more seconds, which felt like an eternity, the nausea went away, and I could fully enjoy the free fall. I began to scream again at the top of my lungs.

"Mali, we're going to free fall a little longer because our body mass is allowing us to," said the instructor. "Is that OK?"

I yelled back, "OK!" and continued screaming.

Fifteen or 20 seconds later he yelled, "We are clear to pull the cord now. Ready, set, go!" I pulled the cord, and the parachute opened, jolting us toward the heavens. Pulling the cord released something in me, and I just let the tears fall. Soon after the parachute opened, I quieted, and the world became still.

The instructor explained where and how to steer the chute. As I pulled slowly to the left, we gently glided to our right, and when I continued to pull without give, slow spirals formed. I was dancing amongst the clouds. I could see the yellow, orange and red hues of the changing leaves beneath my feet. The world looked so small, yet also vibrant and clear. I had wings and was gliding like a free bird. My heart was one with the Universe.

In that moment, a powerful thought occurred to me:

"Could this be what true love feels like?"

That night, Chris and I were still reeling with adrenalin from our individual experiences up in the air. We were also happy to have shared such an adventure together. We went to his house to pick up my car and decided to make dinner there. Afterwards, I went upstairs to grab my backpack and purse. Chris sat on the opposite side of his bed, facing a large window, taking off his socks to get comfortable. I sat on the other side, my back to his, while fumbling around inside my purse looking for my keys.

All of the sudden, I realized how quiet Chris had gotten. I turned to catch a glimpse of him. He was quietly looking out the window. "What are you thinking about, Chris?" I asked.

Without turning to face me, he replied, "I know this is going to sound crazy, Mali, but you have to keep in mind that I'm almost six years older than you and have had my share of dating. And although we have only known each other for three months, I believe I am falling in love with you. In fact, I believe I'm falling in love for the first time in my life."

He turned his head to catch my eyes. I sat there, silent and still, searching for the right words to reply. I swallowed down the lump that somehow materialized inside my throat. He extended his hand. I reached for it and stared at our hands as he sat quietly, caressing mine. A few minutes went by before I found myself able to speak. "Chris, I have had crushes, but I have dated very little in my young life," I said. "I've been too busy trying to do the right things so my parents could be proud and my family could have a better way of life. My heart has been bruised, and I have experienced deep like for other men, but I don't believe I fully know love. I am not ready to say this back. It's too soon for me. I hope you understand."

"I don't expect you to say anything you don't feel," he said. "I just thought you should know where I stand." He took my hand and kissed it. Somehow, Chris trusted my heart even when my mind was not clear.

We continued dating, but he didn't tell me he loved me again after that night, not until I was able to express my love verbally. Two months later, I realized that I loved him. Two months after that, in January, he heard the words from my lips. It was subtly expressed and prior to any sexual context, but it was real and at a time and place where my heart and my mind were at peace with each other.

I learned how to love outside of my boundaries with Chris. I was always a free bird in his arms.

Quite Like This

I have never known a love quite like this,
where all wrongs are forgiven
and all doubts removed
with a quiet look into these eyes.
At a time when my insecurities drowned me,
restoration came upon me,
stumbling as you did when you entered into my life.
I am floating now, with my arms wide open,
free to fall upon your thick blanket of devotion.
Unclouded by the fear of believing in your truth,
I allow myself to behave amorously,
without resistance, forgetting deep, forbidding emotions.
I understand that my fists are not armor protecting the soul;
I know I could never hurt you;
your commitment only allows more space to feel the joy you bring.
The vision you were able to see beyond this moment,
the chance you took by continuing toward me:
these are the reasons for my change of heart.
As the world boldly passed judgment,
it was my path you chose to walk upon.
You have sheltered me endlessly.
I am just beginning to take refuge from the loneliness,
learning to let go of the fear.
I have never loved so openly.

How the Elephant Came to Sit on my Chest

July mornings are so humid in the D.C. area. But not the July morning, five years and 27 days after the July morning I first met Chris. I got up extra early to cook while Chris started a load of laundry. After eight months of living together, we had developed the perfect division of labor. I love cooking, and he loved doing laundry. He enjoyed it so much that he always asked to do mine as well. He relished putting things in order and organizing, which made our home together a sweet and clean place to be. I could hear him giggling in the back room as he spoke on the phone with his older sister, Cheryl, telling her about our plans for the day. He ended the call with "Love you too."

I was making fresh garden rolls. Each roll took at least five minutes to wrap because of the process – soaking the rice paper prior to stuffing it with all the yummy ingredients: cilantro, sliced scallions, sautéed, minced chicken, and cooked shrimp. At that rate, it would be noon before I finished. We were supposed to be at Leesylvania State Park in Woodbridge, Virginia, by then for a picnic with my family. Chris was excited, because this was his first opportunity to get to know some of my cousins he hadn't met yet. We had been engaged for five months and planned to officially announce this to the relatives who had been unable to attend our engagement party in June.

Our two black labs, Shiloh and Sienna, were running around in the back yard. I could hear them wrestling and play-barking at each other. The day almost glowed with an aura of happy normalcy; even the weather was cooperating.

Warm arms encircled my waist as I wrapped another garden roll. A kiss landed on the back of my neck, and a hand snuck around to grab a newly-wrapped roll from the plate on the counter just beyond my stomach. "Hey," I said. "It took me a long time to wrap that." Turning to look at him, I added, "You better savor each bite, mister."

He laughed and started to move his hand to his mouth in slow motion. He took a bite and began acting out what "savoring each bite" might look like. I laughed and hugged him. "Does it taste good, honey?"

"Yes," he said, his mouth half full. "You are the best cook ever! You are the best friend ever, and I just love you."

He put the last bit of the garden roll into his mouth and embraced me, squeezing me so tight that I had to say, "Hun, I know you love me, but I can't breathe." He loosened his grip, and we held each other for a long while. I felt his deep love for me in that embrace. At last, I shooed him out of the kitchen. "Babe, please go take a shower. I'll finish up in the kitchen, and by the time you're done, I'll be ready to head out."

"Yes, I will," he replied excitedly. "I can't wait to play in the water!"

After he got dressed and ready to go, he found me in the laundry room rearranging a few things. "Baby," he said. "I had a funky dream last night. I somehow ended up in a big room where there were lots of people, and as I went around the room, people were telling stories about loved ones they had lost. I saw one particular woman's face. She was so vivid in my mind that it was as if I knew her from somewhere. But I don't. I guess she must look like someone I know."

I had goose bumps. I didn't have a response. I just walked over and hugged him really tight.

When the World Stood Still

Sweet echoes of laughter
Soft kisses upon my face
Memories of a time perfectly blissful
Thoughts of moments
when the world stood completely still.

How I miss those days.

What I would give to turn back the clock
so I can meet you near the lake and run freely
upon wildflowers or freshly-fallen snow.

My dreams continue to take me there.

They lead me to a world I once knew
and slowly ease me into accepting
the world which greets me every morning
as I open my eyes to another day without you.

Chris and I had never visited Leesylvania State Park, a picnic spot on the banks of the Potomac River in northern Virginia. When we turned the corner, we were awestruck by the body of water that greeted us. Taken by its beauty, Chris suggested we stop by the visitors' center on our way out to pick up more information about camping and skiing, and to learn the different hiking trails so we could bring Shiloh and Sienna. "This would be a perfect place to bring our kids ... someday," he hazarded. I laughed at his comment. Chris was never convinced he wanted kids. But after our five years together, he was the one dreaming up our future children.

We parked the car in a lot facing the water. As usual, he couldn't keep his eyes off it. Along the banks, there were larger rocks and green shrubs separating sand from dirt. The river was quite calm at the time of our arrival, and in the distance, we could see a few jet-skis and larger boats cruising along. We took a stroll toward the river. The water gently crashed upon our feet – warm and inviting. Chris grabbed my hand. "It's so beautiful here, Mali," he said. "How come we never knew to come here together before?" I leaned into him and rested my head against his right arm. He smiled down at me and said, "I'm so lucky to have you in my life."

"I love you, too, Chris."

Everyone was happy to see us that day. Congratulations were offered, and I was bombarded with requests to see the new engagement ring on my finger. After a few minutes of introductions and greetings, I placed our spring roll platter on the picnic table, and Chris and I went for a walk along the riverbank to enjoy some alone time before all my relatives arrived. It would be a large group, including Mina's husband Ong and his brothers, sisters, nephews and nieces. Mina had decided to stay home with Hunter, their first child, who was only a year old.

Chris and I took off our shoes and headed toward the river. He was curious whether it would be salty or fresh. We got into a debate and to resolve the question, Chris took his finger, placed it upon the water and tasted it.

"Eew!," I exclaimed. "Stop that, Chris! Yuck!"

He started laughing uncontrollably. "It's just water, honey. It won't hurt me."

I began to look around and pick up shells and rocks. He strolled ahead of me, taking in the sun and looking out into the seemingly-endless body of water. Chris was in his element. I looked toward his feet, and as he took another step, the water washed his footprints away. He turned around to see what I was doing, and I ran to catch up to him with a handful of beautiful rocks. He asked if I wanted to learn how to skip them upon the surface of the river. I nodded, and our competition began. He won every time – even when he tried to mess up so I could win! But every time I lost, he made me *feel* like a winner – with a kiss on my cheek.

When we came upon a historical sculpture of a waterwheel, he read the plaque and commented, "I wonder about the people who were here 100 years ago, fishing for survival in these waters. I wonder about the people who will visit here 100 years from now."

"What made you think of that?" I asked.

"I don't know," he said. "I guess I just wonder about life after we are no longer here. The places we visit will remain, but the people will come and go."

We walked back to the picnic area, and I spread out towels for us to sit upon. I went to grab some water from a cooler, and when I returned, Chris was sitting with his knees close to his chest, his arms crossed and resting on them. He was wearing sunglasses, and his face was lifted completely up to the sky. I watched him take in deep breaths and smile. He was at peace. Therefore, I was at peace.

My brother-in-law, Ong, arrived with the buckets for clams! Chris's face lit up like a kid, and he immediately jumped up from his comfortable position. He walked (well, it looked more like a skip) toward Ong. They shook hands and patted each other on the shoulders. Ong showed him the buckets and the netted bags they were going to use to keep the clams together while diving for more in the water. These two grown men were giddy with excitement.

Ong's nephews, Vincent, Victor, James, Chester, and Tyler, all boys between the ages of 10 and 14, ran toward the buckets and bags. "Let's go, Uncle," they rallied. "Let's go play in the water and look for clams." Chris came over to squeeze my hand and said, "I get to go play now, right?"

I laughed. "Yes, young one, you get to go play now."

With that, the kids (including the two adult kids) headed straight toward the water. I spent the next 10 minutes helping prepare the papaya salad. It would be time to eat soon. Then, I walked over to our towels and saw that Chris had placed his khaki shorts and t-shirt in a bag with my keys and his wallet. Assuming he must have gone to the car and changed into his swim trunks while I was cooking, I walked over toward the fence to see what they were up to. I was pretty far away and simply wanted to observe from a distance.

Chris and Ong were standing waist-high in the water, talking and laughing while the children played nearby, splashing water at each other and being little boys. Within seconds, Chris felt my presence and turned around. He waved at me and pulled up his bag of clams. His smile was huge; I could almost see all his teeth from that distance. He motioned for me to join them, but I held up five fingers. I needed that long to finish preparing something for us to eat. He nodded as if to say "OK" and gave me a thumbs-up signal. I waved and made my way toward my family.

That was the last gesture he ever offered me – a gesture that is forever engraved in my mind. He told me he was OK.

I do not know how much time passed between seeing Chris and the moment a woman, a friend of the family, came running toward the picnic table yelling. I heard her before I saw her. As I turned and found her running toward us, the whole world faded into shades of white, as if a veil fell upon my eyes and shielded them. I don't know what she was wearing. I only saw her in white. "The kids are drowning!" she yelled. "They got swept away by the river current. They boys are drowning!"

I could not feel my feet on the ground but I took off running toward the area where I last saw Chris. No one around me existed. I heard nothing. I felt numb. I arrived at the dock and ran out on it for a full view of what was happening. When I reached the edge of the dock, I saw Tyler holding on to the waist of a man I didn't know as he maneuvered a jet-ski toward the edge of the river bank. I saw Vincent and Victor, or perhaps it was James, on a boat coming back to the shore. I didn't know where Chester was.

When I turned to my right, I found Ong positioned on top of a pylon, knees drawn up to his chest, his head resting on his arms, exhausted and in shock. With his left hand, he held on for balance. He was having a hard time catching his breath.

I heard someone yell, "Where is Chester?" and in that moment, my heart stopped. Chris was nowhere to be found either. I lost my balance and fell to my knees. I sat up, pulled them to my chest and began to rock my body, hoping it would calm my nerves. Everything was happening so fast all around me. People were running back and forth onto the dock, screaming, crying and panicking. I remember a man jumped from the dock into the water to try and help, but by that point, the sirens were drawing closer, and the rescue team stormed the dock. Divers entered the river.

I sat in silence, hearing only the deafening sound of chaos. My heart stopped beating that beautiful Sunday morning. I could not feel my own pulse.

In that moment, with my hands upon my knees, my body rocking back and forth, and the white veil shielding the vividness of tragedy, my heart was ripped out of me and tossed into the river. I knew that Chris was underneath this body of water. I was paralyzed, knowing I could not get to him. I did not know how to swim.

Hours later (or maybe minutes), I opened my eyes. My head rested against the ambulance. A paramedic stroked my back and asked me to take slower, deeper breaths as she held the oxygen mask steadily over my nose.

"Where am I?" I asked. "What is happening now? Did they find my nephew and my fiancé?"

She caressed my hand. "You are in shock, my dear," she explained. "They asked us to bring you to the ambulance while the rescue team continues with their search. I need you to drink more water and take in more oxygen. The investigator will come back to check on you and let you know when your immediate family members have arrived. Your relatives have contacted your sister, Mina, and your mother and father."

"I need to be close to the water," I insisted. "I want to check on the boys and my brother-in-law. I need to be closer to the water." The paramedic continued to stroke my back.

Mina arrived, and my parents followed. When they saw me, my sister collapsed in my arms, and our parents embraced both of us with uncontrollable tears. Ong was being treated by the paramedic team. The boys were given blankets. I walked toward a set of benches, very close to where Chris and I laid our blankets down earlier that day. My parents sat with me – my mother on my left and father on my right. Both held my hands tight. We did not speak for hours as I held back my tears and watched the rescue team move into, above and underneath the surface of the river.

Two hours became six hours, and I did not hear a sound from the people around me as I sat there on that bench with a million questions running through my head: "Why did I invite him to this picnic?" "What will his family think of me for bringing him here?" "What is the probability that he somehow swam to another part of the river, and we just didn't see him with all the chaos?" As each second ticked away, my heart began to empty itself out.

The sun was beginning to disappear into the horizon. In that moment, I remember feeling as if I had fallen with it. The investigator made his way to us. He stood there for a moment, looking out into the river and observing the sun setting with us. Finally, he squeezed my shoulder. His touch triggered tears, and when I turned my head to look into his eyes, the drops fell furiously upon my cheeks. But I did not make a sound.

"My dear, we have to shut the lights off now," he said. "The waters are too dangerous for our team. The recovery will begin again in the early morning. I am deeply sorry."

Not "rescue," but "recovery." It was in that instant when I fully understood and appreciated how one single word can change everything. Yes, I had known for hours that this was a recovery, but it was not until the word was spoken, and I heard it put out there to the Universe, that I truly understood its meaning.

They turned off the lights at 9:17 p.m., two hours after Chester's body was recovered and his immediate family left for the hospital following the ambulance. I was devastated to see Chester, one month shy of his 11th birthday and so full of promise, in that state. We were all experiencing shock, and as his parents and grandparents screamed with pain, all I could do was hold on tighter to my parents' hands and brace myself for the inevitable. I wept for Chester, and the pain was so unbearable that I couldn't feel anything, not even the tears that were streaming down my face. I don't know how many relatives stayed there with me until the lights were turned off. I just know that Mina gently helped me to her car, secured me safely into the passenger seat and drove me home, sobbing. Tears continued to roll down my face but without any noise escaping my lips.

When we arrived at the house, Cheryl, Chris's older sister, was waiting there for me. She had driven three hours from Newport News, Virginia, and was grief-stricken. She collapsed in my embrace, and we cried together. Once we entered the house, I asked my sister to turn on the TV for some background noise; everything was just too silent in my head. Exhausted, I collapsed on the couch and closed my eyes. As my sister turned up the volume, I heard my name – and what followed: "Mali Phonpadith, who is with her family awaiting word from the rescue team regarding the disappearance of her fiancé, Christopher Meehan of Manassas, Virginia …"

I sat up to look at the screen. My sister didn't know what to do. "Leave it, Mina," I said. "Turn up the volume." And there I was, the camera zooming in from the security tape lining the secure area where family and friends had waited on the news. I was sitting there, my back toward the camera, on the bench with my mother and my father.

It was an out-of-body experience, a "Twilight Zone" episode where I felt I was in two worlds. I wanted to reach out and touch the woman in the television. I wanted to hold her and take away her pain. I also wanted to believe she was just a fictional character playing out a part in a very tragic film. It did not register that the woman sitting on that bench was the same person who lived through it and survived to watch it on this screen.

Mina turned off the television and sat on the other couch with Cheryl. I turned toward the glass doors overlooking my back yard and remembered my two dogs. I went through the motion of feeding the labs, crying when I saw them running around in the backyard, not knowing if they could sense what was happening. To this day, I am convinced they knew. That night, for the first time in years, Shiloh jumped onto the bed to lie next to me. I didn't ask her to get down.

My sister lit a candle that night. I prayed for a peaceful recovery the next day and cannot remember how long it took me to fall asleep. I woke up at 5:45 a.m. with a vision of Chris walking shirtless in his swimming trunks alongside the riverbank. He was walking away from me.

We found Chris's body at 1:27 p.m. on July 28, 2003; almost exactly one full day from the time he disappeared. I was grateful the rescue team was able to bring him to the surface so we could move forward with some sense of closure.

I felt the physical pain of this closure. The lights in my world remained off for a very long time.

She arrived that day – the elephant that came to sit upon my chest. The weight showed up the very second I heard the screaming lady running toward me from the river. It felt like a jolt to my body, as though someone threw a brick that struck my chest and pierced the skin. It lodged between my lungs and stuck there, without any way of extracting it from my body.

Once I got used to the caved in feeling, it didn't feel like a brick at all. I had visions of an elephant in my dream, coming to sit on me while I was lying down to rest. The analogy of an elephant was more appropriate. That lazy, slow-moving elephant wanted nothing more to do than to eat at my emotions and sleep upon my heart. I felt no pulse; I had difficulty breathing. Her weight grew heavier after that day, and over the many days and months that followed. There were times in the first three months when I truly felt as though I needed to gasp for air in order to feel anything flow through my lungs. It would take two years before my elephant lost some weight.

Making Peace with the Grief

The months that followed, the steps that I took, the elephant that showed up to sit upon my chest – these things gave me many words with which to fill up my journals. Outside of my family and friends showing up to support me, I needed to find other ways to grieve and to heal. I felt so smothered by care and love that I just wanted to be left alone. I didn't want to pretend to be all right with my family. I didn't want to have to shed (or hide) tears. I just wanted to "be" and I was frustrated every day because I didn't know what "being" meant in this circumstance.

Initially, I dealt with the elephant by simply living with her weight; I didn't have the energy to try and lift her. I was angry but I was more numb than anything, so numb that I couldn't feel anything but the heaviness. Because she was all I felt, and all I knew, I began to take comfort in her presence, and she became a part of me. I was lonely, and my elephant of grief was, in many ways, my only companion. I didn't believe anyone else in the world could understand the depth of my shock and pain.

Because I felt so isolated, I overcompensated for a while by socializing and networking "for business opportunities" every night. I wanted to hear the sounds of people, to fill my life back up with movement and laughter as much and as often as possible, because it kept me from having too much time alone in my empty home.

There were two places I found refuge from my pain. I felt safest to express my pain when I was all alone in the shower and when reaching for my journals to write out the emotions, trying to express how I was feeling in each moment. I didn't talk much about my feelings. I wrote them. Then, I hid them in my dresser drawer so no one else had to feel what I felt. The writing all came to me in the form of poetry and prose, never full stories.

I started to *listen* to myself and began to hear more clearly with each word I wrote. I dreamt of Chris almost every night for three months, documenting his visits each morning as soon as I opened my eyes. I wrote between my coffee breaks and the moment I got home each night. Before long, I began to see myself in a different light as well.

✳ ✳ ✳

Brighter Evening Skies

Nothing has changed
Every day grows longer
The weeks fly away
I place my head gently upon
my pillows each night
I rise to the sun shining
through my window blinds
My heart continues to grow stronger
My strength remains stable
I take refuge
behind the shower curtains
Rinsing my body
Scraping away the pain.

I never imagined
how strong my heart could be.
If I can survive these unbearable days,
I am surely capable of embracing
brighter evening skies to come.

When I wrote, I wrote in poetry about the questions in my mind: Where did my loved ones go after death? Could they hear me, see me, feel me? I wrote about being angry at the Universe and about my questions concerning faith and the meaning of life. I wrote love poems to my loved ones. I just wrote whatever my mind and heart were in conflict over. It was my way of releasing the poison from my spirit, releasing the tears, and letting go of the anger and resentment. I wrote to free myself of negative and unhealthy thoughts. I wrote because writing was the only thing that gave me any solace and peace from the darkness of doubt, uncertainty and anger that things didn't go the way I planned.

It was at least eight months before I could feel the veil covering my eyes slowly begin to lift. Then one day, I noticed I was able to see colors again, this time more vividly. I started to actually listen to every word spoken, including my own. I even began to hear the silent tick-tock of the invisible clock inside my head. But instead of making me race and worry, it actually soothed me. It became a friendly reminder that I should not, and will not ever, take another single moment for granted.

When I was able to accept that my life had taken a different course than the one I set out to travel, I began a new career – one that would allow me to share my experiences and help other families avoid the financial challenges that often accompany grief. I also started to share more of my writing and accepted opportunities to get published, earning for the distinction "Best Poet of the Year" by the International Society of Poets.

The release of writing helped; some of the sorrow left my body when I wrote. But the elephant was still there, a constant, grief-stricken presence reminding me that I was not OK. It was only when I started to truly acknowledge the hurt, the anger, and the feelings of loneliness and isolation that I started actually coping. Two or three years later, I started to face my deepest emotions and allowed myself to cry openly and speak more candidly. *Then*, the heaviness started to lift. I realized that the elephant of grief wasn't there to hurt me; she showed up to remind me that the only way to lift the heaviness was to deal with the pain and find a way to acknowledge, release and move forward. I couldn't bury my pain or ignore my fears. The elephant wouldn't let me (unless I wanted that heaviness to stay forever, of course).

The biggest struggle for me was trusting the Universe again. In the end, coming to terms with the Universe, trusting and knowing that all is as it should be or it would be something else, is the only way to regain forward momentum.

My healing process was tedious and required patience, but the elephant resting upon my chest began, gradually, to lighten her load. She also became friendlier with time. Four years after Chris and Chester passed, I woke up one winter morning and lifted the covers off my body so easily and gracefully that it caught me off guard. I actually said out loud, "Oh my God!" and fell back onto my pillow. "Where did the heaviness go? Where did the elephant go?" I began to cry. I sobbed for more than 40 minutes and made myself late for work.

I was delighted to be rid of her for the time being, yet I wept for the loss – another loss of something to which I had grown accustomed. I was so scared in that moment; I felt free, yet so alone. She had become a friend and a security blanket, protecting me, leading me, slowly and steadily, through the grief that life gives us alongside the joy and love.

Like the elephants of Laos, she existed to protect and guide my journey through any terrain and every kind of weather. But in the four years between that tragic picnic and the winter morning when I realized her work was done and I was free to live and dance and love, I would need her to help me survive several more storms.

PART IV

A FATHER'S DREAM,
A DAUGHTER'S JOURNEY

Happiness is the Only Necessity

Though he is no longer on this earth, my father, like Chris, lives on in everything I do. Paw and I are both such creative souls – introspective, always pondering life and love. Most immigrant parents, especially Asian ones, encourage and sometimes demand their children to go to college and pursue a particular high-earning and prestigious career such as a doctor, lawyer or engineer. My parents certainly encouraged their children to finish school and go to college but they never made me feel I had to pursue a particular path.

In fact, my father encouraged me to pursue my creative side. It was he who heard me singing in the shower when I was 13 years old and asked if I wanted to start practicing with him and performing with a local Lao band. He encouraged my writing as an adult. He knew how my heart lit up every time I told him I had won a poetry contest. He didn't understand any of my poetry because he couldn't read or write English well. But he recognized that sense of passion and, in many ways, Paw lived vicariously through me. He encouraged me to take more chances, to stop and rest more often, to be a little girl and to go play with the butterflies and fireflies outside while he gardened to nourish *his* soul.

Paw and Mai were really proud of all my academic accomplishments. However, I received so many awards over time that it became the norm. They didn't understand what all those certificates and plaques meant but they were always very happy to see that I was accomplishing great things.

Getting straight A's and winning academic contests didn't really excite me, though. What excited me was seeing people's faces light up when I sang to them or read my poetry. My father knew this about me and always tried to find venues – like the Lao Temple, community parties and weddings – where I could go on stage and perform to make other people feel good, to fill them with hope and happiness.

When I told him I couldn't go to Stanford University because they were only offering a half-scholarship, he cried. "I wish I could afford all my children's dreams," he said.

"Paw," I consoled him. "Do I have to be the one to remind you that we are living inside a dream? We are alive! Stanford is no big deal. The University of Maryland will do, and my scholarships will pay for the first two years. We will figure it out from there. By the way, I am going to study to be a doctor."

He cried even harder. "That's not your dream, *nang*," he argued. "I know it's not. You're only choosing that because you're always trying to do the right thing for everyone else. I don't care what you *do*. I want you to choose happiness."

I entered the University believing I was going to become a doctor. After a bio-chemistry class, however, I switched my major to International Business and Marketing. I loved the freedom marketing gave me to create something powerful that touches and impacts others to take action. I could use my right brain as much as my left. I could be creative *and* make enough money to help my family. And *that* made me happy.

"A Father's Touch"

A father's touch upon his daughter's cheek
The waves of hellos and farewells
As he watches me turn my every new corner
I witness him getting older yet lighter
from my positive choices in life.
His little girl grows up before his very eyes.
All his children: vibrantly awake and alive

A magical bond exists
between his wishes and my dreams
His courageous act of guiding us safely inside that boat long ago:
A father's sacrifice equals the opening of doors
Keeping hope afloat
He pushed through screens
believing his children could do anything

With my father's touch upon my cheek
I open new doors
Keep hope afloat
Push through screens
Believe I am capable of anything.

Saibai Jai Means "To Be at Peace"

In the Lao language, my father's native tongue, *saibai jai* means "to feel at peace." Just days before his death in 2006, at the age of 61, my father was asked by our friend Ajahn Noumy, for his definition of life. He said, "To get here to a place where I feel so lucky and feel *sabai jai*."

His wife and children were all gathered around his hospital bed, along with Ajahn Noumy, a Buddhist monk and our guide and counselor during this hard time of parting and peace. Moments before my father shared this beautiful thought, we'd concluded a final discussion with the doctors that confirmed all our fears. As we huddled around in a corner room off the waiting area, it felt as though I was having another out of body experience. I wasn't present inside the moment; I felt I was on the outside looking in – seeing this family completely devastated by the certainty that the man of their lives had only weeks, if not days, to live.

My brother, Soudara, could not contain himself and walked out of the room as soon as the doctors finished delivering the news. He needed some air and space to think. I watched him abruptly open the door and turn the corner. A part of me wanted to run after him, but I knew better. I had been in his shoes only three years earlier and knew the shock of deep loss is unbearable.

My mother remained stoic, maintaining the familiar expression I've seen on her face all my life. She remained calm, swallowed down her tears and wiped away the few that escaped her eyes. I sat there, motionless. I don't know if tears streamed down my face or not. I didn't feel anything but numbness.

But even after this terrible news, with his family gathered around the hospital bed, Paw spoke of peace. And for a few moments, we were all able to forget (or rather, look past) our fear of loss and concentrate on feeling gratitude for the remaining time we had together.

Paw continued to share with us for hours. He was all smiles as he reached out and told us that everything would be all right. He told us he was not afraid. Ajahn Noumy asked us all to gather around the bed and prayed about the importance of fully living life and how the individual paths we are put on and the people we impact along the way lead us toward the wonderment at the end of our journeys here on earth. Holding back tears, my father said he understood the meaning of life well, that destiny led him here and he was very happy to know he did his best for his wife, his mother-in-law and his children.

He spoke of how honored he was to have children he could be proud of. He spoke of our journey here from Laos, and of all the hopes and dreams that danced through his mind as we crossed the river from Laos into the unknown. He said he knew his role in our lives was to lead us to exactly where we are today, and knowing that his mission had been accomplished, he could rest peacefully —and cross into this new unknown.

That night, Lola and Soudara slept in the uncomfortable waiting-room chairs while my mother and I took turns sleeping on a cot inside Paw's room. When she finally fell asleep, I stepped out into the hallway. It was quiet and eerie, with long stretches of rooms and monitors beeping every few seconds. And there I was, walking amongst the hustle and bustle of nurses rushing in and out of rooms. I heard none of it. I just walked up and down the hall, trying to keep some sense of sanity.

Finally, I felt a pang inside my chest. It surprised me, and I placed my back against a wall, slid to the ground and burst into tears. With my face on my knees and my arms covering my head, I rocked back and forth in slow motion.

Less than a week before this night, I had been sitting by a pool in Miami. I was attending a four-day Women in Financial Services Conference and was happy to have a quiet evening before more workshops, panel discussions and my return flight to Washington, D.C. I remember closing my eyes, taking in deep breaths and looking up at the sky. I can't recall what I was thinking about, if anything. I do remember sitting quietly still, wrapping the towel around my shoulders and allowing it to rest comfortably upon my chest as the evening wind picked up. I shifted my eyes from the open sky toward the hotel. From my angle, the architectural genius really gave the illusion of endless windows reaching the heavens. Suddenly, a bright flash traveled across the sky and disappeared as quickly as it had happened. In between two hotel skyscrapers, I witnessed a shooting star grace the Florida sky.

I sat up, feeling an overwhelming sense of awe. I looked around to see if anyone else saw it. I wanted so much to share that moment, but there was no one. The hotel staff members were all too busy with their tasks. This happens a lot in life, I think. When we want to share and celebrate something that moves us deeply, we look around and realize others have their own experiences in life to work through. We have to celebrate such things anyway, even if only with ourselves. So, that's what I did; I even came to the conclusion that the shooting star was just for me that night. Perhaps it arrived as a reminder that miracles do show up from time to time to light up my dark and seemingly-endless sky.

I put a question to the Universe: "My life is about to shift again, isn't it?" In that moment, warm vibrations moved through my body – an answer from the Universe, perhaps? I wanted to believe this was a sign that more positive opportunities for my heart were about to present themselves. I was partly right. My heart's capacity was about to widen exponentially in scope. My life was about to shift again, but was not prepared for what would transpire in the following days.

As I headed toward the elevator, my phone rang. It was almost 10:00 p.m., and my father's number showed up on my caller ID. I answered, "Hi Paw! Is everything OK?" From that moment forward, from the elevator in Miami, to my father's front door, then to the hospital where we heard first, second, third and final opinions, to a heart-sick place where I slumped down in the hospital hallway and wept, my life shifted and events filled with profound teachings drastically changed my views on love and life forever.

When I got home from the conference, Paw opened the door, happy to see that I had arrived safely from Florida. He glowed with excitement, wanting to hear all about the trip. I hugged him and noticed he looked very pale and tired. I asked for an update about his doctor's visit, but they were waiting on more test results. He confirmed that he had been resting all day but still felt exhausted and confessed that the day before he called me in Florida, he coughed up blood and experienced stomach pains. He'd also been having trouble sleeping due to shortness of breath. Finally, he admitted that he was a little concerned about some bruising on his lower back. When he showed it to me, I wasn't prepared for what I saw. His entire lower, left side was black and blue; it appeared to be internal bruising and bleeding.

I told him we needed to go to the hospital immediately, because I felt deep down that something just wasn't right. Waiting for lab results could take another week, and I was convinced he needed to find out what was causing the pain and the bruising.

Paw resisted at first, assuring me that he was just getting old and his body was simply slowing down. Perhaps he strained a muscle at work, he said, and that's why his stomach was bruised and did not feel well. But I wasn't convinced. Several hours later, my mother, my brother and I talked him into going to the hospital. He was adamant about wanting a good night's sleep in his own bed, so we complied with his request to wait until morning. This night would be the last that my father slept in his home with my mother by his side.

The next day, early Monday morning, my brother drove him to the emergency room at Southern Maryland Hospital. After a series of tests and waiting for results, my father's conditioned worsened pretty quickly. He was experiencing liver failure and the doctors were not sure about the cause. They moved him into the intensive-care unit, believing he would have to stay overnight to stabilize his body chemistry. For two days, we watched as my father's blood pressure dropped significantly below the "normal" range and his blood platelets became so low that the doctors asked us to sign papers for blood infusions. He was bleeding internally, and until the CT scan results came back, they could not tell what was happening inside his body.

Finally, on a Wednesday afternoon, two days after we first arrived, and after three doctors had reviewed my father's case, they were finally prepared to share the full picture. My father was asleep when his primary doctor entered to speak with us. My mother and brother were with me in the hospital room. Mina was on her way, and Lola would be arriving from New York the next night to visit with Paw. We had prepared ourselves for decisions on possible surgery or something along those lines. What the doctor shared with us was beyond the scope of my comprehension.

"The CT scan shows a large mass on his liver," he explained. "It has encroached upon the heart, and the lungs have been compromised. We know the tumor is cancerous. There is nothing further we can do here except make him feel comfortable. We contacted Johns Hopkins Hospital on your behalf to see if they have any available rooms. It is a good idea to transport him there for a second opinion and more testing since they are better equipped to handle advanced-stage cancer patients."

We had not been prepared for this diagnosis any more than I had been prepared to see that falling star.

As I sank to the ground in the deserted corridor at John Hopkin's less than a week later, I rocked and cried for what felt like hours. A nurse quietly approached, knelt down next to me and handed me a bottle of water and a packet of Kleenex. I quietly thanked him and immediately noticed his name tag: Jonathan.

Jonathan did not say much, but what he did say shifted me completely: "Take your time here. No one will force you to leave this spot. Just know that you are not alone. There have been many people in this place before you, and many people will show up and cry after you. Just remember, you are never alone." I looked into his eyes and saw deep sincerity and true empathy – not sympathy. He had been in my shoes before. In an expression of gratitude to him, I allowed his compassion to set my tears free. He gently placed his hands on my shoulder and slowly made his way off the floor.

I pulled my head back toward my knees again, and when I was finally ready to look up, the hallway was empty once again – not a single soul, only the strong presence of a guardian angel who left as quietly as he appeared. I smiled and took a few deep breaths, and the elephant shifted her weight a bit so I could breathe more easily. I sat in that position for a while until I heard my father cough. By then, I was ready to be present in each moment with him moving forward. When I entered the room, Paw whispered for me to hand him some water. I helped him take a long sip, and we both grabbed each other's hands, turning our heads simultaneously to watch Mai sleep.

After six days, we decided to move my father to a hospice center. There, his room had floor-to-ceiling windows that overlooked a garden. The first time I visited, he was alone looking out that window. I quietly stood in the doorway, observing him taking in the beauty of the garden as the sunlight danced upon his face. My father loved gardening. I knew he was enjoying the scenery and allowed him his quiet moment of reflection. I stood motionless as the emotions welled up inside of me. My tears had not flowed since the night in the hospital hallway. I did not feel they were ready to flow again yet. My father knew I was there. He knew I understood what he needed, and when he was ready for me to come and sit beside him, he turned his head slowly and gave me an approving smile.

"Paw, are there any specific wishes you would like to share with me?" I asked.

"No specific wishes," he replied. "I know you and Mina will be OK and that you can handle seeing me this way, but I'm not sure I want your younger brother and sister to see me so helpless or in a lot of pain. I feel the most protective of them and I just want you be supportive of them. I want you to take good care of your mother and grandmother. I am so proud of you, *darling*."

I grinned, fighting back my tears, and nodded my head in acknowledgment of his requests.

My father was often in a lot of pain during those final days. Morphine was requested, and hallucinations came and went. My mother and I stayed with him, taking turns resting our eyes.

One night, as we sat there with him, my father moaned. My mother moved to sit next to his bed so she could hold his hands and comfort him. I found myself changing my breathing patterns to take in longer breaths and release them more slowly, as if to breathe for my father. My mother whispered, "Are you in a lot of pain. What can we do to make you feel comfortable?" My father opened his eyes but did not speak. He simply squeezed her hands more tightly and lifted them to caress her cheeks gently and lovingly. My mother buried her face inside his palms. No words were spoken, no tears shed. It was pure love simply expressed.

Hours went by with him tossing and turning. Finally, he exhausted himself and fell into a deep sleep. My mother fell asleep on the left side of Paw's bed, holding his hands while she rested her arms and face on top of his blanket to keep him warm. I held my father's right hand with my left, positioning my body so that I could use my left elbow to hold open my journal and my right hand to write. I was trying to capture all the stories Paw was sharing, the final life lessons he didn't even realize he was giving me. I wanted to catalogue each of his last moments, to capture every second he had left on this earth. I knew one day these words, his words, would be a comfort to me and my family. I didn't sleep that night. I wrote until the sun began to rise. And I was ready to greet my father with a smile when he opened his eyes.

Over the next five days, we took turns staying with Paw so that he would always have one of us by his side. My siblings and I struggled to keep our energy positive and our spirits high in the presence of our parents.

I woke up that Saturday morning at 6:48 a.m. feeling a stronger tightness in my chest than I had felt in a while. It was familiar – the same sensation I felt three years earlier when I ran toward the river, and my chest tightened up, and I forgot how to breathe. I knew without a doubt that this would be my father's last day in this world.

I trusted my instincts so deeply that I called my mother at 6:52 a.m. "Mai, have you been awake or did I wake you?" I asked. "I need to tell you something and I want you to trust my instincts as much as I do."

She was quiet, but I could hear her blanket rustle as she repositioned herself in bed. "I trust you completely," she said at last. "What is it?"

I paused, took a deep breath and continued with conviction: "I woke up this morning with tightness in my chest. I can't explain it but I feel it. We have to prepare and get all the arrangements for Paw's funeral taken care of today. I want him to know we have done everything that needs to be done so he can leave us with the peace he deserves. Mai, please listen and trust me, OK? Paw will not make it through the night."

Mai, Lola, Soudara and Ajahn Noumy stayed with Paw while Mina and I set out to find the right place for my father's service. We drove to the first funeral home, Fairfax Memorial, and immediately felt its beauty and peacefulness. Ajahn Noumy met us there to help us make decisions about Buddhist rituals with the funeral director, who had conducted Lao-Buddhist funeral services there many times before.

Mina had recently bought a collection of acoustic songs that helped calm her throughout this painful experience. That day in her car, a song came on. I can't even remember what song it was now, but it sent vibrations to my fingertips. I told Mina I needed a pen and frantically dug inside my purse for paper, fearing the inspiration would soon leave me. She handed me a piece of paper from the funeral home's marketing packet. That would do. I allowed the words to flow through me and wrote down whatever was being channeled in that moment. By the time the song was over, I had completed a poem called, "Sound of your Laughter." It was the last poem I wrote for my father while he was still alive.

When the song ended, I turned to Mina and asked if I could read her the poem. In the parking lot of the funeral home, I held my sister's right hand while she used her left to turn off the radio and wipe her tears. I read the poem as if the whole world was listening to us honoring our father.

"Sound of Your Laughter"

In loving memory of my father, Sivone Phonpadith

Deep in the night, I can already see your smile
spread across the next day's horizon.
My heart, empty from missing you,
Full, from all the years of loving you.
A kind and brave spirit inhabits me,
lingers on in my memories;
the soft beat and warm flood
of your presence travels gently
through my veins.

Every day will be another
with you still here by my side.
Every evening you will share my every sunset
and you will hear me say "good night."
I will breathe in your laughter
and taste your tears of joy.

My dreams, I am confident,
will allow me to touch your cheeks
and hold your firm hands …
again and again and again.
In my cloudiest of days and loneliest of hours
I will look to the earth, the sky and everything in between
to hear your words of encouragement,
as the sound of your voice
lives forever in my heart.

When the wind brushes against my hair,
I will know it is your touch,
dispelling my deepest fears,
doing your best to take away my heaviest burdens,
leaving only the sweet sound of your laughter
to replace my quiet tears.

As Mina pulled out of the parking lot, I told her my chest was feeling tighter and tighter, and it was time to get back to Paw. At the hospice center, my chest tightened up even more. I didn't want to tell the others I was having such a difficult time catching my breath, so I abruptly left the room, turned to the right and leaned against the wall outside my father's room. I continued to take deep breaths, but it didn't feel like any air was passing through my lungs.

Tears flooded my cheeks, but no sobbing accompanied them. From the corner of my eye, I saw the bright saffron color of our monk's robe travel in slow motion from the entryway of my father's hospice door to across the hall, directly positioning himself across from me. I just stared at him. A smirk formed upon his lips, and I instantly felt resentful and annoyed. I was thinking, "Why in the hell is this supposed spiritual guide smirking at a time like this?"

"Can you describe to me how you feel right now, my dear?" Ajahn Noumy asked.

"I don't know how to describe this intensity to you," I said. "All I feel is numb! It hurts so bad that I can't even feel the pain!" Just speaking about my experience helped my chest to open up, and I began to sob.

Ajahn Noumy stayed present with me. His eyes did not leave mine, and he allowed me to cry as long as I needed. After several minutes of sobbing, I noticed Ajahn gesture to someone coming toward him from my father's room, asking that person to give us more time. My sobbing started to subside into a quiet but intense breathing pattern. His eyes asked me if I was all right. But he waited for permission to speak without interrupting my full experience of releasing the locked energy from my chest. Finally, I nodded.

"Mali, you are one of the most blessed people I have ever met," he said. "This experience with your father and your other recent experiences of love and loss hurt so deeply because you have loved so deeply. You see, my child, you cannot have one without the other. So, you must understand and recognize that this feeling inside of you is coming to the surface because of how *deeply* you love. You are blessed to have the capacity to love this way. It is something to celebrate, so make these tears more about joy and less about sorrow! Find comfort and peace in knowing that your pain is not pain at all. It is your purity in loving that moves you so. You are blessed."

He smirked again and made his way back into the room. I soon followed, without the same intense desire as before to wipe my tears for my family's sake and be strong for everyone else. I entered with my puffy, red eyes. I kept repeating in my head that my tears were those of joy and I was experiencing emotions caused by loving deeply.

That night, my father was surrounded by the women in his life – my mother, my two sisters and me. I read, sitting close to Mai on a chair near my father's feet. Mina and Lola read magazines, each sitting on either side of my father. Around 11:00 p.m., I heard a shift in Paw's breathing. I looked up at my mother and said, "I think it's almost time. Let's gather around him now."

Everything from that point took place so naturally and with very few words among the four most important ladies in my father's life. Lola placed her hand on his left foot. Mina was next to me, holding his right hand and touching his knee. My mother had her hands on his forehead and cheek. And I placed my right hand upon his heart. We all were saying our final words to him in our own soft voices. I told him that I loved him and thanked him for everything he did for us. We all expressed our gratitude, and how proud and honored we were to have had him as our father.

I heard my mother say softly, "We are going to be OK. Be at peace and go now." My hand could feel the last three breaths as his chest moved up and down. The final breath came, and my hand slowly fell with his chest. All stood still.

When my hand stopped moving with my father's heartbeats, I thought about my own breaths. I noticed that the tightness in my chest evaporated and left me as Paw drew and released his final breath.

Saibai jai.

A Father's Legacy: My Work in the World

It was only after my father's death that I truly grasped the purpose of the swift and drastic career change I made after I lost Chris. At that time, I didn't fully process the *why* behind my decision; I only knew the *what*. I wanted to protect lives financially because of what I had been through with Chris.

After he passed away, the mortgage on the home we had just bought together fell solely on me, and all the expenses, from utilities to groceries, were no longer shared. I took one week to plan the funeral in Virginia and another week to travel to Massachusetts, where we buried his ashes in the cemetery where many of his relatives have been laid to rest. The following week, I had to go to back to work.

I had no financial cushion. Chris and I were waiting until after the wedding to get our life and disability insurance policies in place, because I wanted to wait until my last name changed so I didn't have to go through the hassle of changing the paperwork later. The decision to wait cost me so much anxiety, fear and sleep. I had no time to grieve, to process, to feel anything during those first four months after his death.

On December 4, 2003, more than four months after he drowned, I woke up from a vivid dream about Chris. We were walking side by side. I reached out for his hand, but there was an invisible shield between us. I could not feel him. I got frustrated and stopped mid-stride, turned to him and screamed, "Where the hell are you?"

He calmly turned his head, smiled and said, "I'm in a place similar to where you are. There are tons of people and so much to do, Mali. I'm happy here. I just don't want to have to worry about you." He faded away, and my eyes welled with tears.

I woke up to find myself lying there alone in the same bed underneath the same roof that me and Chris shared for several months before he passed away. My tears drenched my pillow, and I continued to cry harder, uncontrollable tears. It was difficult to breathe.

I looked at my clock: 7:30 a.m. It was time to jump in the shower and head to work. But I allowed the tears to continue until around 9:00, when I found the will to get out of bed. I called the office and told my boss I had another rough morning but that I was on my way into work. I had left Unitech two years prior to work for an amazing woman and mentor who helped me see that I was built to be an entrepreneur. I was in charge of account management and business development for the entire Washington, D.C. region of a company that placed high-level consultants in Fortune 500 companies. I enjoyed my role – the flexibility and freedom to manage clients in my own unique way and to offer opportunities to highly-qualified professionals. The work challenged me, but deep inside, I always felt that it was not my true calling.

When I grabbed my towel to head toward the shower, I walked past a mirror. I stopped and stared. The longer I looked into my own eyes, the more intensely I realized I didn't want to do my job anymore.

I had a flashback to early springtime. I was sitting on the lawn in the backyard of our new home. I asked Chris to bring out the lemonade so we could have a picnic outside and enjoy our new home. He sat down next to me, passed the lemonade and kissed my lips. I turned to him and said, "Babe, I have been feeling lately that I should be doing something else with my life other than placing consultants into these corporations."

"Are you unhappy with the work itself?" he asked. "Do you have any conflicts with your boss? Why do you feel this way?"

"I don't know, sweetie. I just feel that this isn't 'it'. I really want to wake up every morning believing that my career is aligned with my mission in life. The problem is, I'm not quite clear yet on what that mission is."

"Well," I said. "We're getting married later this year, and once all of our finances settle from the wedding, I can take on the responsibility of carrying us financially for a while until you figure it out. It will come to you, honey, and no matter what you decide, I'll support your dreams and your life's mission." He raised his glass and made a toast. "To our new lives. To you discovering your life's mission."

Now, I stared long and hard at my reflection in the mirror and thought about my dream. "What am I supposed to do now?" I had asked him. Again, I heard Chris's voice say, "I just don't want to have to worry about you."

That was it! To my reflection, I said, "Well, I think your life's mission has just been revealed, Mali." I was going to sell life insurance. I wanted to represent the voice of Chris for others in the here and now. I would be the perfect person to bridge the gap people have a hard time preparing for, to help them avoid regret about the things they left undone. Having been greatly impacted by the parting of a loved one, and the lack of planning for such a loss, I could share my story and help people put things in place so that they would not have to live through grief exacerbated by financial woes. I wanted to put products in place so people could build the financial foundations they would need in order to get on with the business of healing.

I went to work that morning, drafted my resignation letter and sent it to my boss two days later. One month later, I began studying for my life and health insurance licenses while interviewing with the top five companies in the industry. They all offered me an opportunity to represent their firms. I chose Northwestern Mutual because on all of my interviews, when I asked how each company would help me market and grow my practice, the answer was the same. Northwestern Mutual was the only company that did not hand me a list of people with household incomes around $100,000 and tell me to start cold-calling. Instead, the interviewer there said, "Mali, you came into the business for profound and personal reasons. Naturally, you would start by protecting the people you love … and then ask them to help you protect the people they love." That was the answer I was looking for.

I took off running in my new career, and for two full years, I never looked back. I focused on telling my stories, trying to convince people of the importance of my work and how it would benefit them. I asked for so much trust from the onset. I ran so much and so fast that I didn't realize how far I had run away from my own pain and sense of loss.

I allowed my meaningful work to bury the hurt rather than heal it.
Somehow I believed that every time I told my story, I was dealing
and healing. I told it so often that it became a part of me, something
I had memorized, and while it became so familiar, it also became
far removed from the inner core of me. My story became my pitch,
a mechanical, practiced spiel that shook away the reality. But this
story was not a story; it was an event I actually lived and breathed
through (on the days I *could* breathe). The more I practiced, the less
emotional I became in my presentation. And the more distant
I became, the less effective I was in creating the impact and urgency
to move my clients to action.

My practice suffered that second year. So did my heart. I made
a steady living, but I was not inspiring my clients, and I was not
inspired. My practice felt mediocre and monotonous. How could
I feel anything when I was walking around with a huge, gaping hole
in my heart?

A couple more years rolled by. I met a man named Peter, who
became a friend and then a romantic partner, and I enjoyed time
with loved ones, but I basically went through the motions of
living without much investment. A painful, yet somewhat mutual,
break-up with Peter came and went. Then one day, I found myself
pressed up against a wall in an empty hallway at John's Hopkins
Hospital, sobbing over the inevitability of my father's death.

Sitting on the cold floor that night with my knees to my chest,
I asked myself, "Why? Why is all of this happening? Why so much
pain and loss? Why me, and why these specific experiences in
my life?"

And then I heard my father's cough …

I straightened myself up and made my way into the room. "Are you
all right, Paw?" I asked.

He reached for my hand. The beeping of the monitor was
deafening; yet, his smile took the anxiety away for a moment.
"I just want you to know that it has all been worthwhile," he said.
"My life, the journey, the sacrifices and taking chances – it has been
worth it." As I sat down in the chair next to his bed, my head fell

to the side of his right shoulder, and I cried. For the first time since we learned of his condition, I cried as if I was his five-year-old child again, unashamed of my tears, not trying to hide my sorrow or to be strong, seeking the comfort only a father can give his daughter.

He continued, "Do you know how much you mean to me, Daughter? Do you understand that your every decision in life will impact everyone around you? Understand your worth and one day you will know what it feels like to face death and feel only peace."

I woke up the next day in that chair. My siblings and mother had arrived, and I was planning to head home for a shower and then to check in at work. It had been more than two weeks since I read work e-mails. "And my clients are certain to need me!" I heard myself repeating this phrase again and again on my drive in the office. When I parked and pulled my keys from the ignition, I closed my eyes to brace myself for the barrage of sympathetic faces and caring embraces from my colleagues. I looked from the parking lot to the blinds of my personal office. "Why?" I asked myself. "Why am I doing this?"

I closed my eyes again and saw my father's face. And I heard his words: "Understand your worth and one day you will know what it feels like to face death and feel only peace."

There it was: the *why* for my existence and *why* this profession made so much sense to me in the first place. I am to understand my worth, and from there, help others understand their worth, so they can put plans in place to support and protect their loved ones.

I walked into my office, full of tears from this revelation, and gladly accepted those sympathetic looks and caring embraces. From that moment, I was no longer selling insurance and investment products. My life was no longer just about hard work but rather *heart* work. My purpose in life was not to sell anything to others; it was simply to listen and help guide them to understand their own value.

My elephant of grief was there to help me heal from my father's death. She'd never really left after Chris died and wouldn't leave until I truly came to terms with my emotions following each loss of a loved one. At times like this, with the losses compounding, she felt as heavy as two or three elephants. She accompanied me as I worked and in the quiet moments I had alone. She lent her familiar weight to my grief and slowed me down so I could process and heal.

And one day, I was finally ready to set her free to the Universe again. When I fully accepted that I was finally able to love again, my heart, mind and body found themselves in agreement that I had already fallen in love.

PART V

LOVE AND FRIENDSHIP: A SILENCED HEART UNEXPECTEDLY BEATS

February Thaw

I met Peter in February of 2005, on a cold Thursday night when it got dark before 5:00 p.m. and spring still seemed like a futile daydream.

I sat at a coffee shop in Arlington, Virginia, waiting. The Thursday-night dinner crowd was settling in, and the heat from the fireplace helped to warm my nervous hands. February winds guided me there with my heavy, brown coat and a pink scarf. A waiter came by to take my order. I told him I was waiting for a friend to arrive.

I assumed I could call Peter a friend by this point. Though we had never met in person, we had been e-mailing each other for more than two months. I didn't know much about him except that he was from Paraguay and came here on a work visa several years ago. We struck up a conversation online the previous December about our artistic interests. He was a professional actor, and being an artist myself, I loved everything about theatre and performing arts. As people who came to this country from foreign lands, we both understood the struggle to feel a sense of belonging or home. He came to work for one of the only two Hispanic Theatre companies in the Washington, D.C., area. He knew I was a Lao-American poet who had just started up my own financial practice. Our e-mail exchanges started off very brief and only about once a week. January arrived quickly, and by the end of the month, we were writing each other more frequently – almost every two or three days. Finally, he suggested we meet in person, and I happily accepted. I was looking forward to making a new friend – someone who knew nothing of my recent past, someone who did not recognize me from a tragic newspaper article or the local news story that ran every day, two to three times a day, for almost a week.

Peter and I were supposed to meet that evening at 7:00. He was taking the metro from D.C. and warned me that he might be late, depending on how the metro cooperated. I looked at my watch: 7:07. I signaled for the waiter. I was feeling the draft as patrons entered the shop and thought perhaps a chai-tea latte would warm me up. As soon as the waiter spotted me, a blaring sound rang throughout the café – the fire alarm. It was deafening, and everyone looked disturbed, but no one was leaving. The manager came around to tell us that it was a false alarm and to stay calm. The alarm continued to sound, but everyone around me stayed put, with their hands over their ears and laughing.

I didn't know what to do. Should I head out the door to greet Peter and head elsewhere, or should I stay just wait inside? Within minutes, the police and fire trucks arrived, their sirens now accompanying the alarm system. It was chaos. I held my hands over my ears, hoping the alarm would stop before Peter arrived. This was not the first impression I wanted to make.

When he entered, I immediately knew it was him. He was slender and handsome, wearing a heavy coat, a colorful scarf and a knitted hat. And he recognized me with my pink scarf and hands over my ears. He smiled and shrugged as if to ask, "What the heck is going on?" I responded to the unspoken question with the same gesture, and we laughed with each other from across the room.

He approached me, and I got up to greet him with a handshake. He pulled me closer, gave me two kisses upon my cheek and yelled, "Why isn't anyone leaving?"

I yelled back, "This is apparently a false alarm! We can leave if you want." All of the sudden, the alarm shut off. Again, laughter erupted.

"Well, our evening together just caused a fire alarm to go off!" he said.

I giggled and replied, "I'm not sure if that's good or bad!"

"I don't know either, but you look really nice with your pink scarf." He said, taking off his coat and settling in. His black turtleneck, dark hair and puppy-brown eyes were nice. He was getting over a cold, but I could not tell it by looking at him. We watched as the firemen circled the shop and made their way out of the building. Then he turned his attention to me and asked what I would like to drink. The waiter came by, and I ordered a chai-tea latte. He requested hot chocolate. I smiled at him, finding his selection cute and funny. He smiled back and said, "When I am sick, hot chocolate is my first choice of beverage."

Our conversation started off with typical first-date stuff, mostly about our work, hobbies and interests. We discussed our ethnic backgrounds and shared stories of how we both made our way to the United States. His eyes were curious, but I found myself asking all the questions. I felt more at ease when he was talking and I was listening. His stories of life in Paraguay and his earlier study-abroad experience in the United States were full of color. I laughed when he told me about how he came here many years before as a student, believing that he would end up in those beautiful cities he had seen on television. Instead, he landed on a farm in Oregon. He spoke fast, yet with ease. Three hours rolled by. We laughed a lot. I enjoyed his Paraguayan accent so I kept asking him more and more questions, to hear him speak – and to keep our conversation from directing deeper questions my way.

At some point, he realized that he was doing most of the talking. "I can't believe how much I'm talking about myself!" he said. "I'm going to stop now because I want to know more about you."

Uh-oh. What did he want to know? I had already told him about my work, where I came from and all of my hobbies. What else might he ask? I feared the topic of relationships might come up. I was not ready to share anything along those lines during our first encounter. It had only been a year-and-a-half since I witnessed the death of my fiancé in a drowning accident – not an easy topic to work into conversation, and not something I wanted him to know yet. My solution was to divert his intense gaze. I asked if he was hungry. There was a Thai restaurant down the street that was open late. It was already past 10:00 p.m., but it was clear that neither of us wanted to end the evening. We walked to the restaurant and spent almost two hours talking about everything under the sun. I felt comfortable and so at ease; I couldn't remember the last time my heart was so quieted in the presence of a man who was not Chris. My recent dating experiences had been superficial; they helped to keep my mind occupied but did not do much to ease my heart. But with Peter, I felt safe.

He put down his fork and leaned back in the booth, indicating he was satisfied with the meal. His smile confirmed he was satisfied with the company too. I asked him for the time. When he looked up from his watch, there was a look of shock on his face. "I can't believe five hours have gone by!" he said. "The metro closes at midnight, and we have 15 minutes to close out the bill so I don't miss the last train!" I signaled for the waitress.

With my pink scarf tightly wrapped around my neck and his hat properly in place, he walked me to my car, and we said good night with tender kisses upon each other's cold cheeks. I got inside the car and watched as he turned away and headed off to catch the last train. This was the beginning of a new chapter for me and my silenced heart.

***

"These Early Moments"

The night was kind
Full as the moon and magical.
I looked across the table
Found myself wanting to hear more.
Without many words
I felt understood.

So much left to share;
Not ready to spoil
These early moments,
Wanting only for you
to see me as I am.
Not as things were;
or how they could be.

The Heart's Capacity

From that night forward, Peter and I began to communicate over e-mail on a daily basis. His first phone call a week later was a nice surprise. From there, our friendship continued to grow. We met up for drinks and dinner a few times over the course of a month. Each time, we learned something new about each other and spent several hours just talking. I kept the conversation pretty light and always asked him to elaborate on his answers to my questions. I became a master of evasion. The moment I sensed he was about to turn the conversation to my life story, I subtly and conveniently left out any parts having to do with romance. I suspect he may have noticed my tactics, but his diplomacy and affection for me prevented him from pushing during these sweet, early moments of our relationship.

A couple of days before my 29th birthday in March, we spoke on the phone about my plans for the big day. He asked if he could take me out to celebrate that night. My heart fluttered, which surprised me. I was quiet for a brief second and then without thinking about it further, I graciously accepted. I had not felt that flutter in a long time and wasn't quite sure what to do with it, so I ignored it. I was just spending time with a new friend. I did not believe my heart was ready to move in the direction of love. But as the French philosopher Pascal says, sometimes the heart has a reason that reason cannot understand.

Peter did not have a car at the time since he lived in the city and worked down the street from his house, so I picked him up, and we made our way to a quaint Italian restaurant in Cleveland Park. Walking down the sidewalk, he reached out for my hand. I naturally took hold. It was almost 8:00, but the sky was still bright. I lifted my head and saw that the moon was full. "Do you see the man in the moon smiling at us?" I asked.

He turned to me and said, "How perfect! The restaurant we are going to is called Sorriso, which means 'smile' in Italian." Our eyes met. He winked and squeezed my hand as we made our way through the welcoming restaurant doors.

Over calamari, salad and wine, he toasted to my special day and thanked me for allowing him to share it. Then, he placed a gentle kiss upon my lips. It was as easy as our first meeting at the coffee shop; it felt natural and safe. We spent the evening talking mostly about our family members, particularly our parents. I learned much about his past and saw tender moments of vulnerability when he spoke of his father's passing. I hadn't yet lost my father, but I certainly knew the pain of losing someone so close. Peter was an infant when his father died. He grew up with a stepfather but never had a close relationship with a true father figure. He inevitably took on the role of father, brother, husband and provider for his mother and older sister. This childhood shaped him into a fiercely independent adult. No wonder he could be in the United States for so many years without financial support from his family. In fact, for him, living and working here was the best way to *provide* for them.

Our conversation spilled over into dessert. I took a few bites of my *tiramisu*, which came with a candle for decoration. And then it happened – the moment I had known would eventually come but had been dreading.

"Mali, I have a question that has been sitting with me for a while," he said. "Why did you buy a huge, single-family home with all that land to live alone with your two dogs? How do you manage to take care of it all by yourself?"

My heart stopped, and a flood of overwhelming fear took over. If I told him the truth, he was going to run, like all the other men in the last several months of my dating life, who had asked questions that cornered me into revealing a past they couldn't handle. There had only been a few men, but it progressively got more painful with each disappearing act. I was beginning to really enjoy my new friendship with Peter. I had not felt this safe since Chris and did not want it to end this soon.

I took a few more bites of tiramisu to buy time for my mind to come up with something clever. "Well…," I started. "My sister, Mina, and her husband live just down the street from my house. I saw it as a good investment property and was ready to buy something of my own." I smiled and shrugged my shoulders to indicate there wasn't anything more to the story. I could sense he was not satisfied with my answer, but I turned my attention to the apple tart on his plate and asked if I could try some. Our discussion moved along to his upcoming projects for work.

Later that evening, we drove back to his home. I didn't feel settled as we said good-bye with a warm hug. His question had been sitting at the edge of my heart for the rest of our dinner. I didn't exactly lie to him but I didn't share the full truth either, and that bothered me. I looked into his eyes and felt the genuine affection he held for me. I asked if I could come inside and have tea so I could share something very important. He was surprised but happy not to be parting with me yet.

As I lay next to him on his bed, with my upper body partially embracing his torso, he asked, "What did you want to tell me that was so important? Are you married or something? Do you have kids?" I began to quiver. He noticed, held me closer and kissed my forehead. "What is it? You can tell me."

In what felt like one breath I said, "I don't have kids and I have never been married but I was engaged, and the home I have was once shared with that man."

Instantly, a sigh of release escaped his mouth. "That's it? I'm OK with that!"

"Wait Peter, that's not the entire story. I want to tell it to you now, because if I don't, I am not sure I'll have the courage to share it anytime soon. It's now or much later. Which do you prefer?"

"Now, please."

I took a deep breath and told him about the afternoon in July when my life changed drastically, tragically and in ways that I'm still coming to understand. "So you see," I concluded. "When you asked me earlier about my house, I told you only the partial truth. I moved in to start a life with Chris, and soon after this incident, Mina moved down the street, perhaps to be closer to her grieving sister. I needed to tell you, because if I'm going to have a chance at building a genuine friendship with you, I don't want us to start off with lies."

He fell silent. When he was able to respond, he said, "Oh my God, Mali, I am so sorry this happened to you. I'm so sorry. You are so full of love and light, no one would ever guess this has just happened in your life. I don't know what else to say." Tears rolled down his face, but my eyes were dry. I wiped his tears, nestled my head into his neck and just waited. He silently held me closer. I quietly prepared myself for this to be the last time I would ever see him.

Eventually, we pulled away from each other. I abruptly grabbed my purse and shoes. He, on the other hand, wanted me to sit with him a while longer and hold his hand. I could not look at him anymore. I was fearful that I would shed a tear, fearful that he would believe me to be damaged and broken.

He walked me to my car and kissed my lips with a single peck. "I go away on vacation for a week in Florida with my family tomorrow," I said. "I will completely understand if you want to remain friends, Peter." I smiled, caressed his cheek and returned the kiss. I told him good-bye; he told me good-night and waved as I pulled away.

Three days went by. I had just gotten off a roller coaster at Disney World and decided to check my phone. A text message from Peter read, "Thinking of you. I hope you're having a wonderful time with your family. *Un beso.*"[8] I responded, "*Gracias*, Peter. *Un beso* back." I was glad to hear from him but I did not trust this to be more than a courtesy message at the time. I did not communicate with him much during my family trip. The day before we left Florida, I sent an e-mail expressing my gratitude for his listening ear and my trepidation for having shared so much so soon.

When I arrived back home, I found this message waiting in my e-mail Inbox: "I wanted to tell you that it's OK that you told me about your past. I appreciate the fact that you felt the need to be truthful and open, and I love that. Of course, there is not a chance in hell (sorry for my poetic language) that would keep me from wanting to know you even more. As people and individuals, we are made up of our past experiences, and you are today this woman I've met because of past and present circumstances, so don't be scared about showing yourself as you are. The person who doesn't appreciate that is not worthy of your friendship."

[8] Translation: "A kiss"

The elephant lifted her heaviness from my heart when I slowly went through the process of allowing Peter in after losing Chris shattered it, a heart I believed the elephant was trying to guard and protect by laying her heavy body over it, not allowing anything risky to happen to it again. Somehow, as I started to trust love again (through Peter) she also trusted me to let go of the firm grip, eventually allowing my heart the freedom to beat on its own terms.

In the very beginning, when I began feeling the strong beating of my heart, I felt guilty. One day in the early weeks of our relationship, I cried as I drove home because I couldn't believe I was allowing myself to get close to someone else "so soon." I actually convinced myself to pull back my emotions and told myself that Peter was just an attempt for my heart to confirm that it was never going to be possible to feel the way I did with Chris again.

Thank goodness I did not succeed in squelching my heart. Loving Peter was so important because it taught me about the heart's capacity to hold more than just one love. While I wouldn't love anyone like I loved Chris again, I *would* love deeply again. With Chris, love involved a spiritual, nurturing of self and each other. Loving Peter was all about exploration and new discoveries of self. He became the man who gave me back my heartbeats.

My year-and-a-half-long romance with Peter taught me many great lessons. I learned to allow unconditional love and friendship to help heal my wounds while I still honor the scars. I learned that there are many kinds of love, and it is all right to define each love as we go along. I learned of my own strength and that true love sometimes means setting people free to grow and find their internal happiness and peace. Although our romantic relationship did not grow into a life partnership, Peter will always have a special place in my heart. He and I eventually transitioned into dear friends (but that's a story for later). In fact, he felt more like a brother to me over time. And setting him free to explore his heart and figure out what would provide him with his own sense of peace also set me free.

"Peter's Sky"

In your arms,
my nights do not linger with the unknown
Through your eyes,
my world changes into something grand and kind
I want to leave all my past hurts,
my previous pain, behind
To walk with you and surrender
to brighter, unambiguous skies

Within your embrace,
all insecurities melt away
Upon your skin,
my heart rejoices to the forgotten sounds of its beating
I wish to capture each touch upon my lips
to seal them inside of me
for those long, quiet evenings when you cannot stay

Through your patience and sweet sensitivity,
I have allowed my spirit to breathe deeper breaths
With every gentle kiss you place upon my forehead,
I savor the subtle sounds and smells
of my melancholy days slipping away
As your hand caresses and secures my restless fingers,
I watch each drop of sadness
fade slowly into the night sky.

Strong Hands

We sat in the waiting area of the Washington Hospital Center for more than an hour. Peter didn't say much, and I was going to simply let him be. He sighed deeply – the first sign all morning that he was anxious about the surgery that would remove two lymph nodes in his neck. I sat in a chair connected to his. Without thinking, I reached for his hand, a remembered gesture of affection. He grabbed hold and caressed it. I knew this absent-minded caress meant he was nervous.

I had known Peter for more than five years now; our love had weathered the pain of breaking up four years before, and we had succeeded in cultivating a true, warm friendship. When I heard about his surgery, I was deeply concerned and asked how I could best support him. He initially reacted like a "typical" man and said he didn't need anything, that he would be fine but just wanted to let me know what his doctor had discovered. But after a few weeks of convincing, he allowed me to accompany him.

I looked at him and smiled. All he could offer in that moment was a weak grin of appreciation.

The nurse called out his name, and my heart sank into the pit of my stomach. He got up quickly and reached out to give me a hug and then off he went beyond the double doors. I sat there, with worry, fear and anxiety flooding through my veins. "What happens if I leave and something goes terribly wrong with another significant man in my life? I can't leave the hospital feeling this way! What if he wants me to stay and is too scared and proud to ask me for support?" Because of how much we had shared and supported each other through the years, I felt an overwhelming need to sit beside him and make sure he felt a sense of safety and refuge. I wanted him to know that no matter the outcome, he wouldn't have to go through the experience alone.

I could not get myself to leave the hospital. I tried. But when I got lost and came upon the sign for his surgeon's office, something told me I needed to go back to him. I had a meeting to get to, but something wasn't settled inside of me. He went into the prep area without seeming fearful, but when I saw the sign, a rush of anxiety hit me. It was as if I could feel his energy inside of me. I had to be with him.

I went to the sign-in desk and asked the attendant if I was allowed to go back into the surgery prep area. "What is your relationship with the patient?" she asked.

Without a single thought, I said, "I'm the closest thing he has to family." Without hesitating, she told me where to go.

As I walked through the first set of double doors, I flashed back to my night at John's Hopkins, when I crumbled to the floor and cried for the first time after getting the news that my father was dying. With each step toward Peter, I could hear the silence of that long hallway. As I turned the corner and saw another set of double doors, I stopped in mid-stride. A flood of memories ran through me: the beeping of the monitors, the rush of the doctors and nurses as my father's blood pressure dropped and heart rate escalated. I was paralyzed. I stared at the door that would take me to Peter – afraid to enter and face the possibility that I might have to live through a similar episode. But I couldn't turn back and walk away. Someone I loved was on the other side of this door, and I could feel how much he needed someone close to him. I shoved aside my emotions, walked fast and pushed through the doors.

Inside the prep area, I faced another long hallway. I did not know where to start and how to find him. My heart continued to race, but I took a very deep breath and then I felt his energy to my right. I turned my head in that direction, and there he was, wearing a hospital gown, with his arms crossed over his chest, staring blankly down at his feet. I just watched him for a moment. He looked up and saw me standing there. With a surprised look on his face, he asked, "What are you still doing here?"

"I told them I was your family, and they let me back here," I said. "I just didn't want you to have to be alone."

I pretended to be calm, knowing that at this moment, sitting beside him was not about me and my own fears; it was about offering comfort to calm his fears. I didn't say much; it was too overwhelming. He quietly thanked me. I gently replied with a smile, afraid if I said too much, I would fall apart. And then what kind of support would I be?

Within five minutes, a nurse came toward us with a wheelchair. It was time. He got up, touched my shoulder and settled into the chair. I tried to smile, but the nurse must have felt my energy. She said, "Awww, please don't cry. He's in good hands." I trusted her for some reason.

I sat motionless. He waved, and as I watched her guide him through yet another set of double doors, all I could do was look up toward the ceiling and say, "Please, God, do me a huge favor and promise he really is in good, strong hands. I'm not sure I can do this again, but if I must, then give me strength to become those hands for him."

The surgery went well. He was released the same day, and I went to visit with him later that night. He was grateful to have my unconditional friendship. I was grateful to be in a place where past hurts no longer impacted my ability to continue a relationship with someone who had come to offer me so much. I realized just how far my heart had come – from being utterly shattered to strong enough to love without boundaries.

"Filling Up the Trust Jar"

My words flow through paper – travel across the wires
Release themselves from my body – at times like wild fire
I am passionate, impulsive, yet I slow down to enjoy each mile
No need for me to run and hide this time;
You will be staying here for a while.

I see you in the distance, supporting me from afar,
Content to have your own set of wings and dreams
Yet, with each new step,
I feel you closer and closer from where you are.

My words, your actions –
How we have learned to communicate.
Quite naturally, somehow, our spirits can relate,
Choosing to share without boundaries.
Release us of any unrealistic ties
A love without expectations, a trust from lack of lies
That place in your heart, this empty trust jar,
… is filling up with millions upon millions of happy fireflies.

My Heart and Her Recovery

I decided five years after Chris passed away and two years after Peter and I broke up that I was no longer going to date. Rather, I would be open to meeting extraordinary men. As soon as I made that decision, my heart began to feel calmer about the idea of love entering my life again.

Three weeks later, I went dancing with a few of my girlfriends from college in the Adams Morgan district of Washington, D.C., a popular area for eclectic night life. We stopped at an Irish Pub, and as the alcohol was flowing, we decided to stay there and dance the night away. My friend, Amy, wanted a picture of the entire group, so she searched around for someone to take it. There was a tall, slender gentleman standing behind me with his back to us. Amy tapped on his shoulder and asked him to take our picture. When he turned around, all I saw were his piercing, blue eyes. Actually, they were not exactly blue. They were blue, green and hazel – a combination of vibrant colors.

Our eyes locked immediately. He smiled and gladly agreed to take our picture. My girlfriends noticed our quick but poignant exchange of glances, and seeing as though I was the only single girl amongst us that night, they seized the opportunity to embarrass me. After five or six different camera snaps, this gentleman was finally off the hook. Or so he thought.

As Amy took the camera back, she asked, "What's your name?"

"Matthew," he replied.

" Thanks Matthew. I'm Amy and *this*," she said (pointing directly at me with a wink), "is my friend Mali."

"Oh my God," I thought. "How embarrassing! Why the wink that he could witness? Not at all obvious, right?"

"She's amazingly wonderful," Amy continued. "Multi-talented, speaks a gazillion languages and she's totally hot. Don't you think she's hot?" She giggled, noticing that I was shriveling up and looking for a rock to hide under.

Matthew was a great sport. "Yes. She's beautiful," he said, and seeing the mortification on my face, he began to laugh too.

Amy wasn't through yet. "Where do you think she's originally from?" she continued. "I bet you'll never guess! No one has ever guessed it right the first time!"

"Oh my God, Amy! Will you please *stop*!" I gasped out loud.

He continued to laugh, looked quizzically at my face for a few seconds, which felt like forever, and said, "Laos?"

I was stunned. "WHOA!" I said. "That's the first time anyone has ever guessed on the first try!"

We spent the rest of the night talking and dancing. He didn't leave my side until the bar closed. For the first time in a long time, I met someone who showed up as his authentic self. He continued to show up just as himself as I got to know him. Matthew never had any walls up when it came to his emotions. He was truly expressive when describing his feelings and sensitive and confident enough to communicate openly. It was refreshing, because his sincerity allowed me to mirror him – to just show up as an open book and be myself.

He e-mailed me the next day, and a true friendship emerged through our virtual letters. He lived in Pennsylvania and was recently divorced from a lady he had loved since college with whom he had a young son named Andrew. A writer at heart, he worked nights with a graphics and public relations firm, and spent his days with his son and his poetry and stories.

Matthew came to visit me several months later. We met for coffee at one of my favorite local book stores, Kramer's Books. We shared a chicken quesadilla and laughed and talked for hours. After five months of sharing our stories, our first "romantic" dinner felt wonderfully safe. I enjoy the intense butterflies in my stomach when I am interested in someone romantically, but what I cherish most is the ease with which two people can share time together when they don't have to worry about pretenses or putting up any facades. I love feeling safe enough to be my true self.

✳ ✳ ✳

That night was the beginning of our brief but beautiful romance. Over the following five months, we continued to communicate via e-mail and phone calls. I visited him twice, and he came to me three times. He was a sensitive soul and brilliant when it came to data recall. He knew random answers to trivia on everything from American History, to stars and galaxies, to pop culture, that no one else I knew could guess, except, perhaps, for my godfather, Mac. In fact, Matthew and Mac were so much alike. Most of all, I adored their shared pensive and quiet nature.

And Matthew adored me. He admired my passion for life and supported every hope and goal I ever shared with him. He was my source of encouragement, my confidante and unconditional cheerleader. He was my equal intellectually. In time, it became apparent that he was, in fact, my mirror. I saw the depths of my own joys and sorrows, hopes and dreams through his eyes.

Reflected in the light of his eyes, I saw myself saying exactly what I wanted to say, doing what I truly wanted to do, sharing everything from the depth of my soul. I could finally hear my heart as it spoke to me about what made me feel happy and at peace. This clarity was not so much a realization that my heart could actually beat again, but rather that my heart was fully processing and making clearer decisions on what she wanted to hold, carry and release. I was no longer on cruise control, in my life or my love life.

In early December, as I was reflecting on my wonderful relationship with Matthew, a strong and powerful realization came over me: Matthew and I were not meant to be life partners. I can't even put into words why I knew this was true, but I knew that it was. Matthew, in essence, was a beautiful, sturdy bridge for my heart to walk across in order to make it safely to the other side, a place where healthy and peaceful love can exist, a place of strength where my heart was finally whole again.

The year came to a close, and Matthew came to D.C. to attend a New Year's party I hosted with some friends. I decided to be present with him, to enjoy our night together and embrace how amazing and wonderful this man had been for me.

The next day, we were living in a new year. As we walked down the streets of D.C., holding tightly to one another's hand, I knew my heart would always hold love for him, but I accepted that our paths would lead us down different roads. I held him a while, kissed his lips with what felt like hundred little pecks, stared into those beautiful eyes of his and said, "Good-bye Matthew."

A few days later, we had "the" conversation on the phone. He also understood that we weren't right together long-term. We were both sad but neither of us was angry.

Matthew found his true life partner two years later and has since gotten married. When I heard the news, I felt an overwhelming sense of joy, knowing he has followed his path to happiness and peace.

Matthew taught me not to judge what I need and want out of life, to just show up as myself! With Peter, I was elated to know my heart could actually beat and feel again. But with Matthew, my heart was not just *feeling* deeply; she was actually able to process *what* she felt, and I was able to start making healthy, good decisions again. Matthew was yet another beautiful firefly that entered my atmosphere, one to grab a hold of, nurture and learn from. Then, it was time to set him free.

"Kisses Upon My Brow"

My heart is breathing slowly and steadily these days.
Unfamiliar with the sound of your laughter,
it listens with quiet curiosity.
The mornings are clearing;
the nights draw warmly to my new being.
I now greet the soft moonlit evenings with open arms –
no longer afraid that the moon will expose my tears.

Your fingertips trace the outlines of a cracked spirit;
they caress the wounds and remind me that wounds, in fact,
make up the beauty of my complicated heart.

Can you cherish all of my idiosyncrasies?
Embrace my nervous laughter
and challenge me to show long-forgotten tears?

I am free – more alive and much lighter
than the morning dew upon my window sill.
You are here – to remind me that life moves on and soon,
sunlight will be peeking above the horizon to accompany
your kisses upon my brow.

PART VI

TRAVEL STORIES:
ADVENTURES IN LOVE AND
THE WORLD

"The Hour's Breath"

Time moves.
How much I have changed
with little subtle shifts of the wind.

The heart continues to beat.
My spirit feels lifted from the deep sleep of despair.

I await the morning glow,
excited to know my path is no longer covered
with the mist of grief.

I can see clear across the ocean now.
Blue skies and bright moonlit nights;
The clock moving at a pace I can agree with;
enjoying each moment
of the hour's breath upon my back.

What the ATV Taught Me About Letting Go

The golden sun pressed gently upon the Pacific Ocean. My younger sister, Lola, screamed in my ear, 'What are you doing? Put your hands back on the steering wheel!'

I laughed hysterically. The ATV was on cruise control for all I cared; I was releasing my spirit to Costa Rica. It was February of 2007, not even a year after my father passed, and the last couple of years had been so full of locked-away pain as I constantly put on a front to protect everyone else. I was tired of carrying such a heavy load upon my heart. I was tired of being selfless.

Mal Pais, a tranquil village spread out along five kilometers of road in the southern part of Costa Rica, is a beautiful location to get away from it all. My sister, too, was escaping the routines that accompany a broken heart. The rustic sounds of monkeys jumping from tree to tree and exotic birds calling from the bushes comforted our souls. At night, I would sit on the balcony and listen to all the new wonders of nature. Some sounds were unrecognizable, from animals I never knew existed. Yet, I was there, living inside a new reality.

I went into my darkest corners during my meditations in Costa Rica, a place where I felt so at peace and in tune with my environment that I felt safe to revisit those troubling thoughts. I listened to myself and the world intently and rediscovered places I had buried through the years. This was the beginning of my new beginning.

In January, Lola asked me to accompany her on a vacation to Costa Rica to celebrate her birthday. Then she paused and added, "If celebrating is even possible the way I feel these days." I did not give the escape more than a minute's thought. I needed to go somewhere sunny and warm. I needed to feel something (anything!). I was upset with life once more. How could the Universe do this to me – break my heart over and over again? I was just getting back on my feet from my breakup with Peter. I was scared and still reeling from the trauma of losing my fiancé and then caring for a dying parent. I no longer had the capacity to carry any more pain. I had reached my breaking point.

$$* * *$$

Our small commuter plane took off from San Jose, the capital of Costa Rica. My sister was looking beyond my shoulder toward the ocean shores of the countryside. I could feel her heart beating, and her curiosity overshadowed my thoughts. I was relieved to know that her heart was working. I didn't quite feel mine yet, but I followed her gaze out the window of the plane. The view was breathtaking: aqua-blue water, endless greenery and the mystery of a new place ready to greet us.

Once we landed, a friendly driver was there to meet us, eager to show us our home for the week – a little house named Casa Lisa in the tiny beach town of Mal Pais. Surrounded by what felt like wild jungle, Casa Lisa was quaint, earthy and rustic, without any modern-day appliances and with very little clutter; it was beautiful, just what our hearts needed.

The house was a long walk from the next town, stores and restaurants. The roads were not paved, so traveling by foot was not as convenient as we had hoped. But when the manager of our rental property stopped by later that afternoon driving an ATV, we learned that renting one was the best way to get around this little town to explore. I was a little nervous at first. I had ridden on an ATV but never driven one. He convinced us that managing the vehicle wouldn't be difficult, and the next day, he gave me a quick driving lesson.

Within five minutes, I was ready to go. Lola hopped on the back seat and wrapped her arms around my waist, and we took off to explore the beach. Everything was so green, and the winds felt like living and breathing souls. The sun felt warmer in Costa Rica; its shine penetrated my soul. My heart began beating – wildly and freely. The harder I pressed the accelerator to move us forward, the more I felt my pulse trying to break through my chest. I experienced a sense of freedom and impulse like I had never known before. As we rode along the ocean, my heartbeat fell into rhythm with the waves crashing on the sand.

That afternoon, we drove to and from the nearby town three or four times. The roads were made of gravel. The grocery stores were family run. Everything about the town was rustic and pure. I felt utterly connected to nature the entire day.

By mid-afternoon, we finally stopped at the house to rest and enjoy settling in. While Lola explored the jungle outside our door, I freshened up with a cold shower in a bathroom built to allow guest to feel one with nature. It was made entirely of stone except for a glass ceiling, which allowed the trees and animals surrounding the house to get the full view of me while I enjoyed them in their natural state. As the sun beamed through the glass above me, my bare body truly felt connected to the earth.

Alone with myself, I cried deeply that afternoon in the shower. As the water cleansed my body, it also washed away so many emotions. Earlier that day, the energy of Costa Rica pressed up against my being, unlocking doors I thought were nailed shut. The doors were pulled wide open; the flood gates crumbled. In the shower, I pressed my palms against the wall in front of me, grounded both feet and allowed the pain to escape through my lips.

I stayed in that position for almost an hour while I released the deep pain of living through unanswered prayers, lost hopes and abandonment. I thought of all the physical and human aspects I missed about those I truly loved and gave my whole heart to; I could no longer see my father, feel Chris's lips against mine, hear Chester's laughter … all these emotions poured out through my lips and tear ducts.

That evening, Lola and I decided to tour our neighborhood on foot. The sun was about to go down, and we put on our summer dresses to greet the Costa Rican sunset with style. As we walked down the gravel roads, dirt tickling our toes and the winds caressing our calves with the hems of our dresses, I felt my spirit, once missing in action, now accompany me with each step. I took note and began counting each breath. When we got to the beach, we took off our flip flops and continued on the soft sand to the ocean. We were minutes away from the golden hue disappearing beyond the horizon. I found a big piece of wood to sit on while Lola walked further along the waterline studying sea shells. I studied her, wondering if her heart would find all its pieces one day and wishing the same for my own journey.

She pointed toward the ocean. I nodded with a smile and turned my attention to the setting sun. I continued to count my breaths, and when the sun sank beneath the sea, I was relieved to feel my heart still beating. Somehow, life always goes on, I thought. I rested in the beauty of this knowledge and began trusting in life's eternal persistence.

Suddenly, I heard my sister's voice close to my ear:
"Are you OK, sis?"

"Yes," I said. "Believe it or not, I am more than OK." We both smiled that smile, the one that half bleeds while it rejoices. She took my hand to lift me from the sand, and we made our way back to the house for a celebratory dinner. It was her birthday after all. I felt like it was mine too.

That week, there were moments when time stood still for me, patiently waiting for me to catch up. I had coffee with the hummingbirds and butterflies every morning, toasted the moonlit nights, stared out into the open skies and tried to count the endless stars. The stillness of my spirit and the natural sounds of life called me back to my core. The refuge of Costa Rica filled the moments of meditation in which I allowed myself the freedom to let my tears flow and opened me back up to seeing the beauty of the Universe again.

During our final full day, I forced Lola to learn how to drive the ATV. We were on our way back from the beach, and I asked if she wanted to drive. She paused but then quickly shook her head. It was in the pause that I heard what she was really wanted to say. That was it – she was driving or walking.

At first, she kept stalling the engine while laughing nervously. Finally, I held onto the steering wheel with her, and she immediately felt more at ease. Slowly, with each mile, I loosened my grip and eventually let go. She was a natural. It didn't take very long (less than two miles) before she was pressing harder on the accelerator. I saw in her body language what I felt deep inside. It was time to sit back and press that accelerator. It was time to GO. I tightened my grip on her with my legs and put both of my hands up in the air. I trusted her to get us home. I learned to trust, and re-trust, many things while I was in Costa Rica – like my heart and the Universe.

"Her New Release"

Breathing freely –
she released the elephant that once sat upon her chest
as she traveled many difficult roads,
each putting her through a series of tests.
Colorblind to gray skies,
no longer a part of the peripheral view,
she let go of all the fears
of each insecurity she once knew.

If the heart could sing out loud,
the words would chime freedom and peace.
Her chambers open to explore and dance,
ready for her debut – her new release.

She cannot wait for others to be ready,
cannot miss the wonderful chance
to flutter and be discovered
when life decides to offer
yet another beautiful circumstance.

No moment is ever appropriate
when so much is at risk.
As every hour slips away,
the clock steals another perfect kiss.
Reach for her or allow opportunities to be forever lost.
She cannot wait any longer –
her love is worth more than such a cost.

Finding Laos in South America

When I think of Paraguay, my first memory is the warmth in every household that received me when I visited in June of 2008. While my grasp of Spanish helped, I would have understood everything they offered me – hospitality, friendship, family, love – without any words at all. My friend, Marcela, and her family made me laugh, cry and sing. One night, we even danced around in the living room laughing so hard we couldn't breathe (a long story with bananas).

Marcela's grandmother – a fellow poet – and I became fast friends. Within 30 minutes of meeting me, she was searching her entire room to find a gift that I could remember her by. I joked that she should wait to give it to me on the day that I would be leaving her – which was still six days away! But she wouldn't have it; she did not want to forget and certainly did not want to be forgotten! She gave me a pen, with which I could write down what my heart wished to explore. This pen had a calendar, and she asked me to remember the day we met, the day we shared stories about our past loves and our hopes for a lifetime filled with more love.

Marcela, her aunt Gildy, and her cousins, Celeste and Ricieli, showed me around all the neighboring towns. On our way to each new place, we looked for a chiperia alongside the roads. *Chipa* was the perfect winter morning snack – a warm, doughy dish filled with wonderful cheeses that melt in your mouth. There is no denying that I came back from my South American adventure with a few extra, wonderful pounds. I tried every traditional Paraguayan dish that exists, except for the bori-bori (perhaps that was meant for my next trip). My shape got a bit more round than I prefer; yet, I could not justify any guilt or regret for having tried such delicious foods – *mbeju, gnocchi, sopa paraquaya, milenesas, lomitos arabe, chorizos, chipa guazu,* barbecue meats of all types, a *la parilla and empanadas.* Totally worth it!

On the first three days of our stay in Paraguay, the five of us women drove cross-country from Asuncion, eastbound passing the towns of Caacupe, Coronel Oviedo and Ciudad del Este, toward the port of entry into Argentina. It took more than five hours of sunshine, rain and fog to arrive at this port, where a ferry would transport us inside our car across the river – a 15-minutes ride into Argentina.

But we ran into trouble at the border. Apparently, there was no one "official" available that day to stamp my American passport and allow me to depart Paraguay and enter the neighboring country. We were stunned, disappointed and upset. After trying (unsuccessfully) to negotiate for almost 30 minutes, we finally came up with a story we felt sure would tug at their heart strings and persuade them to make an exception – my Argentine boyfriend was to meet me at the Falls of Iguazu the next morning for the purpose of proposing marriage! Not being able to get to our meeting spot was simply unacceptable, especially after having traveled from the United States for this wonderful chance of finding "true love."

It was a compelling plot, beautifully presented by Marcela's aunt, who asked us to stay quiet in the car so we didn't screw up her story. I was thankful; I would not have been able to keep a straight face throughout this negotiation. We did get some sympathy from the ladies "patrolling" the border, but it wasn't until we gave one of the workers a $5 bill that the official stamp somehow made its mark upon my passport – just in time for us to make the ferry.

The next morning, after a very cold night in a single hotel room with four other women (where we ran out of hot water within the first hour of checking in and the TV only received strong reception for one station), we made our way to the Iguazu Falls, or *Cataratas del Iguazu* as they call it in South America.

The immensity of the place nearly defies description. I was there one early, foggy morning, and after the peaceful train ride through the wilderness surrounding the Falls, I could only describe the serenity of my spirit by saying it was like being called by thunderous yet melodic sounds of grandeur as the tremendous water plummeted more than 269 feet at the rate of 553 cubic-feet-per-second. This place is called Devil's Throat, or *Gargantua de Diablo*.

I could only say over and over again, "*Que impresionante!*"[9] My body and spirit felt as if they were out of my physical shell; it was as if I was looking at this place inside some distant dream recalled from another life. I could not believe a sight like this actually existed in our world.

[9] Translation (from Spanish): "How impressive!"

It was a magical experience to stand alongside the rails, holding on tightly, closing my eyes, lifting my face toward the early morning sunlight and allowing myself to listen to the rhythm of my own heartbeats pounding in sync with the Falls of Iguazu. Walking away, I felt I was being sent back to *life* ... again.

Our next stop, Posadas, Argentina, was the whole purpose of our road trip. My father had passed away two years before. Soon after his death, I visited our family friend, Ajahn Noumy, the Buddhist monk who provided spiritual care for Paw (and our entire family) in his final days.

Again, he shared his wisdom and spiritual guidance with me, helping my mind and heart understand that life is a cycle, and somehow, everything is interconnected and everyone has a purpose and contributes in some way. He reminded me that my father's energy will always remain a part of my world.

After finding some solace, we discussed my passions and my love of world travel. I told him that I had never been to South America, but it was on my list of places to explore. He mentioned that he had been involved a few years before with a journey to bless a newly-built Lao-Buddhist Temple in Posadas, Argentina. "Why in the world would there be a Lao Temple in Argentina?" I asked.

He told me that Argentina, during the Vietnam War era, opened up their borders for refugees. Roughly 200 Lao families were accepted into the country and relocated to Posadas. Eventually, the community of Lao families raised enough funds to build their own temple. That day, I made a mental note and a spiritual commitment to one day visit this community of Lao-Argentines and these their sacred temple.

Two years later, I was on my way. After the magical and surreal experience of the Iguazu Falls, we drove another five hours past endless farmlands – taking pictures of every single cow, which were of every possible size and color you can imagine. The three girls, Marcela, Riciele, and Celeste, sang "Color Esperanza" while creating seated dance moves as I filmed and re-filmed their choreography. The windows were down, and my hair flew around as I fumbled with the digital camera, a cup of traditional South-

American infused drink called yerba mate in hand. Laughter and music chased away the minutes. Before we knew it, the sun was starting to set, and we finally reached the sacred grounds of the Lao-Buddhist Temple of Posadas.

When I stepped out of the car and planted my feet upon the Earth, an energy traveled up through my legs, my chest, my heart and tear ducts. I smiled and then I cried in wonder of how small the world truly is and how beautiful life is meant to be, if we can only choose to see it more often in such a light. The orange glow of the sun crawled slowly toward the horizon, allowing me to see this place with my twinkling eyes, to touch the sacred doors of the temple, to take mini-breaths and savor the fresh air of Argentina – and the fresh air of life.

The groundskeeper greeted us in perfect Argentine Spanish. I placed my hands together and bowed my head to greet him in Laotian. "*Sabai dee*," I said.[10]

He smiled in acknowledgement and began to speak to me in our native tongue. He told me that the head monk was away from the temple, conducting a special ceremony for a Lao family in Cordoba. Bizarre as it seemed to know that there were Laotians scattered throughout Argentina, I had to remind myself that it is this way all over the world. It hit me in that moment that my life could have landed me anywhere in the world. And for a brief second, I reflected on the fact that my life's course could have easily ended on the day my parents escaped with me and my siblings across the Mekong River into Thailand. My chance to see Paraguay and Argentina, as well as the rest of the world, is simply a blessing in itself.

We eventually made our way from the temple to the nearby community of Lao people. My Internet search had confirmed such a neighborhood existed. Our guide drove us, and we weaved around in circles for a while, not fully sure we were heading in the right direction. Then I spotted two Asian children walking in the streets. We stopped to ask if they knew where the Lao people lived. It was a bit surreal to hear myself asking them in Spanish, and even more bizarre to hear the boys answer back in fluent Argentine accents.

[10] Translation (from Laotian): "Hello. How are you?"

I explained that I came all the way from the United States to find the temple and this Lao community and asked if they could take us to the small prayer house so I could give thanks for a mission accomplished. They gladly accepted the request.

When we arrived at the prayer temple, everything was locked up. To our astonishment, one of the boys told us not to worry. His grandmother had a key; he would lead us to her home to request her assistance. What were the odds of that happening? He led us a couple of blocks from the temple to his home. His grandmother was at the store, so we waited. No more than five minutes later, two women approached slowly and greeted us kindly in broken Spanish. "Hola," the older lady said.

"*Sabai dee, Mai Thou*," I responded, using a Laotian term for addressing any elderly female who is not immediate family.[11]

She looked a bit puzzled. I explained that I had traveled all the way from Washington, D.C. to find the small community of Lao families resettled in Argentina. I wanted to know that the story I read on the Internet was true. I shared how grateful I was that the journey led me here and asked if I could enter the prayer room to give alms and thanks for this overwhelmingly emotional experience.

The two women were excited and honored to open the doors and show us around. They sat with us, speaking Spanish to my Paraguayan friends and Lao to me. The most amazing part was that these two women were both from the same town where I was born. How in the world did the Universe provide such an experience for me?

When we finally drove away from the neighborhood, I sat quiet and still. I could not come up with the words (in Spanish, English or Lao) to describe all the emotions that ran through me. My thoughts were jumbled together and my heart yearned to understand what just took place inside of it. There were too many happy "coincidences" for my journey to have been anything less than fate.

---

[11] "Mai Thou" is the Lao word for "grandmother" and is also used to address any elderly female who is not immediate family.

Then, I heard my father's voice telling me that all things in the

Universe are interconnected. It was as though he heard me when I lit the candle inside the temple and prayed for his peace and eternal happiness. I was more certain than ever that he had been with me all along, not only in my dreams, but in these waking moments. I felt my father's presence with every step from the United States, to Paraguay, to the *Cataratas de Iguazu*. He was with me as I drove away from Posadas, toward a life where I could now accept and fully embrace that all things are exactly as they should be. I was able to see the beauty in each step, how all the little things make up the whole of everything. It was an awakening to realize that I have everything I need to find that internal sense of peace. I realized that I can find "Laos" wherever I go, because I can always look inward and come home to myself.

Over the next few days, we remained extremely active: visiting the Jesuit Ruins of Encarnacion, going on a shopping spree for souvenirs in Asuncion, touring the artisan towns outside of the capital city and spending several days visiting with other members of Marcela's family, whom I had come to love and who had grown to love me.

On my last day in Paraguay, I felt melancholy as I packed my suitcase, trying to fit in all the souvenirs and storing away, in my own head, every beautiful memory we created here. I did not feel quite ready to leave this country. There was still so much left to explore. I felt it calling me to stay a while longer; yet, I believed Paraguay was confident in letting me go, as if she knew I would return to her one day.

"Peace Through Travel"

Across from you, sometimes miles apart
I see a space inside your eyes
filled with wonder, curiosity for the meaning of life
Clear, blue skies across the ocean
A place beyond the sunrise
where love and peace serendipitously collide.

You wear your hair different from others
Your skin changes to a darker shade than mine
Our hands close the gap between bruised fingers
The heart knows nothing of space and time
You are here to stand beside me now.

Peace comes to sit with me through my travels
As I carry your vision – that space inside your eyes
May you walk the lands I continue to uncover
Communicate in a language of our hearts' desires
I will rest and stay with you … even in oceans wide
Where love and my peace serendipitously collide.

PART VII

MY WHOLE HEART:
FULL OF FIREFLIES

A Sense of Family Outside of Family

As fate would have it, I have been blessed with a second Mom and Dad – my godparents, Jean and Mac. Back in 1979, Jean placed the deciding vote at Davies Unitarian Church to sponsor my family's immigration to the United States. Thanks to her vote, we were able to travel across the ocean, solidifying a place to call home, and a lifelong relationship with her and her husband.

Because my parents worked so many long hours, Jean and Mac often stepped into a parenting role for our entire family. They coordinated doctor's appointments, taught me how to drive, coached me through my first job interview and worked tirelessly to create a sound emotional and financial foundation for us.

When I was 19 years old, I wanted so badly to study abroad and feel like a "normal" college kid – a kid who had choices to explore in life. But I could not leave without a United States passport. I was a permanent resident, but with my refugee status, I did not have travel documents. I was no longer a citizen of Laos because my family fled the country. And I was not yet an American citizen either. I was in between.

Mac and Jean helped me study for my citizenship exam. The day I got sworn in, Jean drove me to the Immigration and Naturalization Services office in Baltimore. It was an emotional day for me. I now had a place I could officially call home. I became an American. A few days later, we got a call confirming that my passport had been expedited; I could travel with the University of Maryland's study-abroad program. I couldn't believe one of my dreams was about to come true!

Mac drove me to Washington, D.C., to pick up my first passport. My heart was filled with butterflies. That pocketsize document symbolized a world of endless possibilities. For the first time, I felt a sense of home. This was my ticket to go wherever my heart wanted to take me and an assurance that I had a country to which I could return, one that would greet me with open arms (or at least let me into the country).

Mac, in his quiet, observant way, took my emotions in and owned them. He squeezed my right shoulder lovingly, and in that moment, I knew he was a proud papa. "We need to celebrate your first official week as a U.S. citizen," he said. "And now with your passport, you are a 'citizen of the world' as well."

Through my giddy smile, I said, "Lead the way!"

That afternoon, Mac drove me all over town. He was one of the smartest men I will ever know. This isn't an exaggeration. He had one of those minds that could beat anyone in a good game of Trivial Pursuit. He loved history especially. We stopped at every monument in the city. Each time, a group of people formed around us, assuming Mac was my personal tour guide. My heart smiles just thinking of that moment and all the moments he was a part of my life.

We ended that day at the top of the Washington Monument. From this high place, he pointed out the different buildings and explained their history. He taught me a lot that day about architecture, the layout of the city and the significance of citizenship. But most of all, he taught me about a love without limitations, which simply feels through each experience with pure emotion. He taught me that to be a "family" doesn't require sharing DNA. He chose to love me with his full heart, as if I was his daughter. And in my heart, he was my father.

In April of 2005, when Mac's cancer had come and gone and then come back again, I sat beside his hospital bed on his last night as a citizen of the world. I was alone with him while Jean went home to rest before a church event that night. His last words to me were, "You're special, Mali. You're stronger than you realize, and your entire life will be full of blessings. You have been a blessing to my life. Please take good care of Jean for me." Tears rolled down my face. I held tightly to his hands, leaned closer to him and whispered, "Yes. I will take good care of her, just as you have taken good care of me." I fed him his meal and kissed him on his forehead, and we smiled at each other as I closed the door behind me.

Several hours later, Jean called to say that Mac passed away peacefully in his sleep. I felt at peace with our earlier good-bye. In that moment, I reminded myself how important it is to say what our hearts need us to say – without letting another moment go by. "I love you, Jean," I said. "I will take care of you. That's what Mac asked me to do, and I am honored to do it. You won't have to walk through this alone." Jean and I continue to walk together through many beautiful and painful experiences.

My relationship with Jean and Mac has gifted me with so many awakenings. They taught me that philanthropy and community service are not just about monetary contributions; it takes so much more than a full wallet. Their lasting lesson to me was that giving to and thinking about other people are among the best ways to create a fulfilled life.

Jean's single vote changed my life, and quite possibly saved it. My family and I made our way across the ocean, because someone else wanted a hand in creating the beautiful journey of our lives, before they even met us in person. They gave us a real chance. They taught me that hope, belief and love are all I need. Mac and Jean represent all these things for me. I want to live my life representing these things for others.

Mac and Jean's kindness proved that a single soul, with one single act, can change the world. They have certainly changed mine.

Rafael: True Friendship Transcends

I tapped on his shoulder. He slowly turned around with a look of annoyance. "Excuse me," I ventured. "I forgot my Spanish dictionary today. Could I borrow yours for a moment?" Without a word or any expression on his face, he reached into his backpack and handed the dictionary to me.

I kept it until the end of class, and when it was time to go, I tapped on his shoulder again. "My name is Mali. What's yours?"

"Rafael," he replied, sullen and haughty.

"Thank you, Rafael. I really appreciate you lending me your dictionary."

He nodded. I was curious. Why was he so distant? I tried to engage him more by asking if he was from Maryland. He told me he lived in Maryland, but he was born and raised in Costa Rica. I started laughing. "So you speak fluent Spanish and you're taking a Spanish class?" I asked. "Jeez, you're going to mess up the curve!"

Finally, an amused smirk appeared on his serious face. "It's Spanish Literature," he said. "And besides, when you grow up being taught Spanish by your parents, that doesn't necessarily mean they are teaching you grammatically-correct Spanish. I love literature and art and I wanted to learn more about Spanish literature."

"Oh, I see," I said. "So, I can cheat from you regarding the concepts of literature, and you can cheat from me with respect to proper grammatical structure."

He laughed then – a genuine laugh. And the ice was broken. As I walked out of the classroom with him, he asked about my major. I told him I was shooting for a triple major. I came in pre-med but once I took the bio-chemistry course, I decided I did not have enough passion for medicine to go through anything like that again. My first year of college was spent mostly on general studies, so I did not lose too many credits when I decided to study International Business in my sophomore year. I also decided to pursue a Marketing degree and continue with my Spanish studies.

He seemed quite impressed. I had passed a test. His nonchalant demeanor intrigued me. Why isn't he as excited as I am to make a new friend? Almost as if this was an interview, he seemed to take detailed mental notes on every word I said.

I told him I was headed to the business school. He was going toward the architectural building, which was close by, so we walked together. I didn't bother asking if I could join him on the stroll. He didn't say much, so I made the decision for both of us.

I told him that I, too, was born overseas and filled him in on some of my family history. I guess knowing about my journey made him feel some sense of connection to me, because he began to open up.

"I came to America as a teenager," he told me. "My mom was here all along trying to work and raise money to send back to my family. A few years ago, she was finally able to bring us here to study. It's different here. I don't have many friends, and people don't really understand or accept me. I'm Latino and I happen to be black. I find most people don't know how to place me. They treat me like an 'African-American,' and I don't even know what that means … to be treated like an African-American. I just know that more often than not, it doesn't make me feel good."

While I didn't expect to hear all of that during our five-minute stroll, I listened gratefully. I was happy to let him speak and to see him let his guard down.

Rafael and I took hundreds of strolls together after that day. We naturally grew in our friendship. Nothing was ever forced. I showed up to every class that year, and he was always there to greet me, always prepared with a story to lift my spirits and energy.

We spent many nights throughout college on the phone. I worked full time and was a full-time student so I didn't have much time to date. I always made time to share my heart with Rafael though. After I got home from work and ate dinner, I would call him to find out about his day before I started on homework. It was usually about midnight by the time I could focus on my studies.

Somehow, our conversations always came back to what real and hopeful love might feel like. We would describe how our beloveds would look, how smart, funny and attractive they would be, and how much they would adore the heck out of us. Our time together always included food, followed by a long stroll, and then chatting it up with music playing in the background. He loved opera. I was more into acoustical pop. One thing we both loved was how music always lifts the spirit. He never allowed me to leave without singing something to him. I think he was the only person in the world who appreciated my singing that much.

Rafael shared so many deeply-rooted fears with me. He told me that he was abused as a young child by a relative. He never told me who, and to him, it didn't matter anymore. What was important was that he could say it aloud to someone without having immense fear that he would be judged. He cried so many tears over that – over so many things.

One afternoon during our junior year, Rafael walked with me to class. I could tell he had something on his mind. "Mali," he said (with his accent, however, it always sounded like "Moeli"). "I have something I have wanted to tell you for a very long time. I just don't know how. Can we meet after class on the fourth floor of McKeldin Library?"

I was concerned but decided not to ask any questions. I nodded. He gave me a hug and rushed off to his next class.

A couple hours later, we met in the front entrance of the library. "It's such a beautiful day out, Rafa," I coaxed. "Why don't we sit outside while you share whatever it is you need to tell me?"

He shook his head. "I really need to tell you in a more private place," he said. He was so anxious I could almost hear his heart throbbing a hundred miles a minute. I rubbed his back, and we made our way to the elevators.

The fourth floor was the quietest floor. There were no community areas, therefore, no noise of students socializing as they pretended to focus on their curriculum. This floor was filled with hundreds of bookshelves with a few hidden coves throughout for students who wanted a remote place to focus.

Rafael led me to the very back corner. We found a small table with two chairs facing each other. I sat down; he started pacing. "Rafa, please just sit and tell me what's going on!" I said.

He was sweating now. Finally, he sat down and took a few deep breaths.

I reached over to grab his hand. "Just tell me."

Tears welled up. Another deep breath followed. "Moeli, I have never shared this with anyone before. I'm so afraid you will walk away."

"Rafa, don't be ridiculous. That will never happen."

"Moeli, I am gay." Tears fell from his eyes. He held his breath.

I was so relieved. "Well jeez, Rafa, I thought you were going to tell me you were dying or something. What's the big deal, babe? Somehow I already knew and was just wondering how long it would take you to figure it out for yourself! Besides, my cousin is gay, and I adore him."

He was in shock. He couldn't believe it. He smiled. "Dammit, Moeli! I have been walking around for months with anxiety and fears for nothing! *Carajo!*[12] We both erupted into uncontrollable laughter.

Apparently there was a mad scientist in the making, working around the corner from us. She came to our table and asked us to shut up. "*Mierda!*[13] Do you think she heard our conversation?" he asked.

"Rafa, *mierda* is right! Who gives a shit?"

More laughter. We grabbed our bags and ran toward the elevators so our scientist friend wouldn't call the quiet-police on us.

---

[12] "Carajo" is a Spanish curse word that loosely translates to "damn."
[13] "Mierda" is a Spanish curse word that loosely translates to "shit."

Rafael had a deep fear of abandonment. This entered into his consciousness at a very young age, when his biological father abandoned his mother. He never really knew this man, only his name and where he lived. He told me once that he wanted to write him a letter or show up at his doorstep to ask why he left, or at least express how his father's actions (or lack thereof) shifted his entire existence and belief system. It was painful to watch Rafael struggle, using many things (mostly relationships) to fill up that huge hole in his heart.

His romantic relationships were plentiful. Those many characters always found a way to impact his heart, but there were only a select few men who profoundly impacted his soul. Those who actually made a difference in his world were the ones who exercised patience and trusted that underneath all those insecurities and fears, there lived an amazing spirit in Rafael, one that longed to feel accepted.

How perfectly aligned we were. Empathy and love kept us together. There were moments throughout our friendship where I was in so much pain that I might have shattered into a thousand pieces had he not been there to literally pick me up from the floor. And the same was true for him. I have never shared so much of my inner self with anyone the way I expressed it with him. I trusted him, because he trusted me. He was a wonderful mirror of imperfections. I didn't feel alone in the world while he was in it. I always knew I had a place of refuge; one of the safest places I have ever known was by his side.

While we spent so much time together describing the kind of hopeful love we always wanted for ourselves and each other, I am realizing now how beautiful and hopeful our love for one another was. Life does this – gives us everything we wish for, and somehow, we fail to see much of it until it has passed. We overlook such things because we wait for them to show up in the perfect packages we envision. There is no perfect package, no perfect love; there is just love.

I learned a lot from Rafael in the 14 years that we shared our journey together. I learned that pure and unconditional love of the soul can exist, and this kind of love sees no color, feels no barriers and leaves no room for judgment.

I have experienced the kind of grief that accompanied the tragic accident with my late fiancé and nephew. I have lived through the grief of watching my godfather, Mac, and then my own father pass away after their battles with cancer. Each experience impacted me differently. I felt moments of guilt. I struggled through self pity. I meditated through days and nights of deep sorrow. But I never fully embraced anger with any of those good-byes.

Suddenly, anger entered my life like never before as I was again brought to my knees.

It was mid-September, and I had returned two nights prior from Lewes, Delaware, where I officiated the ceremony for my friends' (or more like my sisters') wedding. The day was peaceful and beautiful. I will never forget the experience – the sound of the waves crashing behind me as I married two beautiful people, celebrating life and love.

Earlier that morning, I made time to meditate because Rafael had been on my mind for the past week. Rafael was supposed to be my date for the wedding. He wanted to support his best friend with such an important role. But I hadn't spoken to him since two Sundays prior. I asked him to let me know by the Wednesday before the wedding what time his bus from New York City would arrive in Washington, D.C., on Friday night. I was to pick him up, take him to stay with me that evening and then leave really early Saturday morning for the beach.

I text-messaged him Wednesday night but got no response. I reminded myself to call him the next day so we could work out our logistics. But his phone was out of service. That surprised me, but I wasn't disturbed. I knew Rafael had been out of work for several months due to the economic conditions. An architect, he was finding it difficult to get freelance jobs, or any jobs for that matter. Perhaps his phone was shut off because he wasn't able to pay his bill in time. I would send him an e-mail instead. "Surely, New York City has free internet cafés he could visit," I thought. "He's probably going to send me an e-mail soon." I went to bed that night and slept soundly.

Friday afternoon: no word. I decided to call his mom, Amanda. *"Hola,* Mama. Have you heard from Rafael this week?"

"No, I think the first time I spoke with him was two Sundays ago." she said. That was the night of our last conversations as well. I told her he was supposed to be my date for the weekend wedding, but I hadn't heard from him about his arrival time that night. She knew about the wedding. He had mentioned wanting to get new shoes to wear with the Lao shirt I gave to him for his birthday in August. "He told me he was excited about it," she said, "and that he would try to see me if it was possible for him to stay until the Monday after the wedding. But I haven't heard from him in over a week."

My heart sank. I told Amanda I would write him another urgent e-mail asking him to find some way to communicate with us by this weekend, or we were going to call the police. That Saturday morning, I drove to the beach without him. I called his cell phone three times that day, hoping to establish contact. Nothing.

Meditating before the ceremony allowed me to calm my senses and shift my energy back to where I was – about to take part in something sacred for two people I loved. Magically, I was able to center myself long enough to be truly present for their wedding ceremony.

During my drive back Sunday night, my anxiety grew more intense. The road signs telling how far to Washington, D.C., showed fewer and fewer miles while the clock in my car continued to increase its number. I couldn't calm my fears anymore. I had distilled them all weekend long, assuring myself that my anxiety was from my past traumas and unexpected tragedies. But surely there was no possible way anything horrible could happen in my life again so soon. I did not trust that my intuition button worked anymore.

I called Amanda. "Mama, I have a very bad feeling sitting in pit of my stomach," I said. "I have not heard anything from him. Have you?"

"No, mi hija."[14]

---

[14] Translation: "No, my daughter."

"Amanda, I need you to call the police station and ask them how to contact the New York police. We need to tell them that no one has heard from Rafael in over a week." She was starting to panic now. "I don't know what else to do, Amanda," I said. "This is not like Rafael. In 14 years, we have never gone one week without speaking or communicating somehow. My best friend would never stand me up for an event without telling me why. Please call the police."

"OK, Mali," she said. "I will." It was already 10:00 p.m. when I spoke to Amanda. The local police contacted the New York City Police Department and told Amanda they would be in touch with her as soon as they had an update. Amanda was so frazzled that, when she got off the phone, she realized she did not leave them her phone number.

All day Monday, we were all so unsettled. I couldn't sleep the night before. I couldn't eat without feeling nauseated. I was also upset with myself for allowing my fears to control me so much.
Of course, I never truly believed something tragic had happened. What were the odds of one person, in the span of six years, experiencing *five* tragic losses? What were the odds?

By Monday night, Amanda could not take it anymore. She and her sister, Ruth, decided to take a bus to New York City. They would leave at 3:00 a.m., hoping to arrive at Rafael's apartment by 8:00 – before he had a chance to get started with his day. Perhaps he was just in a depression over his job situation and his most recent romantic heartbreak. Or maybe he just wanted to take a break from the world and be by himself.

Amanda needed to be sure. We all needed to know. She called me Monday night to tell me her plans. I asked if she wanted me to go with her, but she said Aunt Ruth would be with her, and they would be fine. "Wait for my call tomorrow morning," she said. "I will let you know when we arrive."

The first thing I remember Tuesday morning was staring at the clock. I don't remember even falling asleep. At some point after 8:00, Amanda's number popped up on my cell phone. I sat up on the edge of my bed.

"Hola, Mama …" Before I could say anything more, I felt a hot flash throughout my entire body. I began to take deep breaths as I listened. I couldn't really make out what I was hearing at first. "Hola! Amanda?" My heart began to race when I recognized the sound of her sobbing uncontrollably.

She cried for what felt like a million hours. I let her, swallowing down a knot the size of the Universe. And then I heard, "He's gone." My body slid from the edge of my bed and onto the floor. This was not possible. "The police have been here since last night. There was police tape surrounding his entire floor and there was no way for them to contact me prior to me showing up."

"Oh my God, Amanda," I managed. "Oh my God! What happened?"

"They found him asleep in his bed. No trauma. They believe he swallowed a few bottles worth of various antidepressants. They are telling us it was likely a suicide." Then she lost it again.

"Mama, I love you," I said. "Please let me know what you want me to do right now. What do we do now?"

It didn't make any sense; it must have been a mistake. My best friend would never even consider such a thing as suicide. He was the light in every room; his laughter echoed in all our ears even after each party subsided. There must have been a mistake! And yet, when his mother said the only words I can recall that week, "He's gone," the world stood still once more. My heart was without a pulse for what felt like hours. I remained as calm as I could for his mother, telling her that I would come be with her for however long she needed me. *"Te quiero mucho, Mama. Estoy aqui como siempre mama. Estoy aqui."*[15]

---

[15] Translation: "I love you very much, Mama. I am here, as always. I am here."

"I will call you later today," she said. "We need to get more information from the investigators. They are still going through the apartment and making sure there wasn't any foul play. By the looks of it, the apartment was locked and bolted from the inside. No forced entry. The officers had to break through the window to enter. Why, Mali? Why? *Mi* Rafa! *Porque, mi* Rafa?"[16] I told her I would wait for her call and if she needed me to drive to NYC, I could be there by early evening.

I hung up the phone, called my sister, Mina, and a few dear friends to share the devastating news. Then, I shut off my phone completely. For the next several hours, I sat on the floor, my back against the bed, looking into the full-length mirror that was perfectly positioned in front of me across the room. I just sat there looking at myself and not recognizing the person staring back. I felt numb. As the tears flowed, the rest of me was silent – a familiar sound. I don't remember how or when I got up off the floor.

Amanda returned to Maryland the next day. The investigators told her there was nothing she could do until the coroner's report was completed. More than a month later, the report confirmed the investigator's theory – suicide. The news was beyond devastating.

And then there was anger. My elephant was back but this time with a vengeance. Forget sitting around on my chest all day; she was in full stampede this time. She entered my heart in a mad rush, tearing up trees and moving the earth, gouging out a river of tears, as if she did not get enough attention the last few times grief entered my life. I was angry for so many reasons.

---

[16] "Porque" is the Spanish word for "why."

I had many spiritual conversations with Rafael in the first few months after his passing. "How could you do this to me when you have watched my heart shatter into so many pieces?" I demanded. "How could you lie to me about your anxiety and depression? How could you betray my trust? How could you not have trusted *me* to help carry your pain? How could you abandon me without saying a word? How could you give up on us – all of us? How could you give up on yourself?"

Yes, I was angry, deeply and furiously angry. It was all about me, about how much he hurt me.

After a while, the anger started to subside a bit. Perhaps my elephant was getting tired. Soon, guilt showed up to take its place. I struggled even more with this one. I blamed myself for not being a good enough friend, for not instilling enough trust that he could turn to me. I blamed myself for not paying more attention to him. How could I have not seen any signs? We'd collected all the empty pill bottles in his apartment and found medications indicating severe depression and bi-polar disorder. How could I not have known he was bi-polar? How, after 14 years? How?

Learning to forgive others is so challenging; learning to forgive yourself takes even more strength and courage. When the anger and guilt overwhelmed me, I found ways to keep my sanity. I created lists upon lists of all the great things we shared, the wonderful memories he gave me and the ways in which I had been there to support him. These everyday reminders and exercises were what eventually allowed me to breathe again. I came to accept that my best friend loved me like he loved no one else; he gave me everything he could, shared what he felt he needed to share and protected me in ways no one else would even understand. I came to accept that I could not have loved him more than I did and that his suicide was not about anyone but him. He was not looking to hurt anyone in his life; he simply wanted his peace.

*** ✳ ✳ ✳

I was asked to read the eulogy at his funeral. Sitting next to his mom in the church, holding back my tears to focus on wiping hers away, I was determined to get through the experience and make him proud. As part of the eulogy, I shared how we met and what he meant to me. He was not just my best friend; he was my soul mate and my brother. And I read a beautiful card he sent to me in July of 2009, when I finished my collection of poetry. The voice was no longer mine but his, and I finally heard what he was telling me all along: "Share light; spread hope; live out your dreams. I will always be here for you."

He waited excitedly for more than six years for me to publish my book. Well, he no longer needs to wait for his copy. He will, instead, live inside of it forever.

"Rafael"

It was wonderful to hear from you, old friend
We simply continued where we last left off
This time you were sad
but next time you will feel much better,
and again, we will laugh at the silly things
our hearts put us through
We will never grow old; we will never be strangers
It is too easy to call up the memories
You laugh and I sing
You cry and I philosophize
about how the world will make sense
when all is said and done
And when we are all said and done,
I will await the next time our hearts collide.

Marcela

In addition to my sisters, Mina and Lola, my life has been blessed with a peppering of soul sisters. Marcela Ferlito Walder is a young woman with whom I am honored to share this bond of sisterhood. Six years younger than me, Marcela looks at me as an older sister, and I see her as a talented and spirited younger sister. She relies on me for advice, and I rely on her for a different perspective on my own life. She keeps me on my toes and helps me to laugh a lot and stay youthful.

Marcela is petite and slender with large, brown eyes that can see through to your soul. Her positive spirit, sense of humor, and naïve, yet cunning way of expressing herself constantly charms me and creates a space for us to be together – whether we are in a room full of people or miles away from one another. I understand her jokes and am sometimes the only one who howls with laughter alongside her.

I met Marcela through Peter, who lived in the basement of her parent's home. When he and I were dating, Marcela and I bumped into each other from time to time at the house, but we never communicated except to say "*Hola*." Peter had his own entrance through the back gate, so it was rare that I saw Marcela and her parents.

Peter also worked for Marcela's parents' theatre company. In addition to acting, he supported them on administrative tasks and technical support, as a production assistant, and whatever else they needed. I first visited the theatre for their spring production, in which Peter played a suave South-American gentleman who needed assistance passing on to the afterlife. We had been dating for three months but it was still a surprise to me when he officially introduced me to Marcela and the other volunteers as his girlfriend.

They all welcomed me with open arms, but there was a sense of distance with Marcela. It was as if she didn't trust me, or at least the situation. I promptly volunteered to do anything they needed. Marcela was very open to my offer. She led me to her mother, who put me to work as an usher.

✳✳✳

After the show, I met Peter outside of his dressing room, and we headed out for a late dinner together. "Peter, you were brilliant on stage tonight," I told him. "I'm surprised you guys don't have more volunteers there to help!"

Peter shrugged. "Volunteers are hard to come by," he explained.

I remembered how frantically all the volunteers had been running around before the show and felt that, perhaps, I could help more. I kept seeing Marcela's face. There was something about the way she reached for my hand and led me to her mother that made me feel a deep affinity for her. And there was something very sad in her eyes that night.

Peter always drove with his left hand on the steering wheel and his right hand holding mine. I squeezed his hand. "I think I'll sign up as a volunteer then," I said. "I feel you all need my help, especially Marcela."

He turned his head and said, "Really? You want to help us?"

"Yes. Peter. I'd like to help. Is that all right?"

He quickly leaned in for a kiss.

A couple months later, when I went to pick up Peter for dinner, Marcela answered the door and embraced me with an intense and warm hug – as if she hadn't seen me in months. "It's so great to see you again," she said. "What have you been up to? You haven't been here to visit for several weeks. I was worried that you guys weren't together anymore and I'm really happy to see that you're back." I was taken aback by how familiar she seemed to feel with me, but also humbled by the warmth of her embrace.

It wasn't until Peter and I officially parted ways that the bond between Marcela and I proved itself to be stronger than I had imagined. We became inseparable. Though Peter and I reconnected eventually, that summer I felt the keen loss of my friend and lover, but I did gain a sister in Marcela – and another family. Her parents basically adopted me. After my father passed away, her family constantly offered to support me in every way possible. I ate many

* * *

dinners at their place when I needed time away from my own family. This family became my refuge, a place where I could laugh through the tears.

And to this day, when I am with Marcela, she makes me laugh until it hurts. My favorite thing to do with her is to just sit, talk about random things and tease each other over hot herbal tea. When we go out to restaurants or stroll around D.C., she always brings out the inner child in me – the one who forgot how to laugh, dance and be carefree. We skip, jump and flirt with the cute boys who walk by. Being in her presence is like letting down my guard, letting my hair loose and treating life like a sandbox, where we get our hands dirty while enjoying the blissfulness of each new moment. She brings out my free spirit.

Marcela is an artist at heart. She sees things very vibrantly and is eternally curious. Her mind is always going, and her imagination helps to keep the artist in me fully awake and alive. More than anything else, she just lets me be. Through the most painful times of my life, she has offered to sit beside me and have slumber parties until my tears dry and I can close my eyes to rest. Her youthful way of going through life keeps me positive through darker days. She is one of my fireflies I have collected and held close to my heart.

"Melodies"

I listen
as my bare feet enjoy
the sweet caress of white sand.
This face smiles upon sunlight
taking in the new glow
of what once ... slipped from my hands.
She has reclaimed herself
by trusting time ... and entrusting ME once more.

She beats freely now
to the sound of new music
I have been writing.
Calmer evenings and brighter mornings,
as she hears soft melodies
reviving her from deep sleep.

I am no longer alone for she is no longer afraid
to dance with me again, through windstorms and rain.

New sounds all around me
bring hope and joy to my days and nights.
Noise from the past now intertwines
with peaceful stillness...
full of purpose
for my extraordinary, new life.

Misti

When I need a reality check – to get encouraged or called out – my soul-sister, Misti Burmeister, is just the friend to do it. She's poignantly honest and once she knows she can trust you, she is fiercely loyal in return.

Misti and I met in the spring of 2004, at very vulnerable times in both our lives. She had just moved to the D.C. area and was feeling lost and alone. She was in the early stages of her coaching and speaking career, and I was still in my first year of practice with Northwestern Mutual, feeling the pressure of building a new business. My heart was still heavy as I learned how to live with the emptiness of Chris's absence.

At our first meeting over coffee, I spent most of the time telling my *full* story, which was, and still is, rare for me. Misti was kind and genuinely intrigued when I told her about my tragedy and how it inspired me to change career paths. With my clients at Northwestern Mutual, I was always matter-of-fact when sharing my history, providing a high-level, Cliff Notes version of my tragedy. With Misti, however, I found myself pouring my heart out to someone I had just met. It surprised me how my story flowed from me, not mechanical or rote at all.

Although I knew I was talking too much, she made me feel safe to share what I needed to share. Typically, I perform this supporting role for others. I rarely spend time talking about myself. Instead, I prefer to ask a lot of questions and listen to other people's stories. I recognize this as a defense mechanism, a way to distract myself from my own pain and hide my hurt from others. But with Misti, defenses crumble, and there's nowhere to hide. That day, she truly created a space for me to be myself, with all my elephant-sized scars and firefly-sized hopes.

Time flew by that day, and I barely got a chance to learn much about her before we both needed to leave. I could tell volumes, though, by just being in her presence. Misti has a brilliance about her, which is made even brighter by her vulnerability and fueled by immense strength and a touch of anxious fear. As she spoke, so animated (and underneath, so nervy), I found myself sitting across the table from her, looking into a mirror. I left our meeting feeling less alone in the world. There was someone out there who was just as scared as me about the concept of starting over in life.

Like Rafael, Misti is the kind of friend who challenges me, who stretches me beyond illusionary limits. She once told me that I take too long making decisions; I'm too careful and stay inside my comfort zone more often than not. No one ever told me that before her, and at first I was hurt and offended. But the simple fact that her words impacted me so much indicated it was something I needed to ponder. I reflected on all the big decisions in my life. She had a point. There were many opportunities that I let slip by because I wanted to wait and think before taking risks.

Misti not only challenges me to grow, but she also knows how to celebrate all the wonderful things she sees in me, including my ability to find calm in the midst of turmoil. While she immediately recognized my calm, she didn't understand at first that solitude is crucial for me to maintain this inner peace. When something profound or painful happens to me, I need to shut off all noise; I turn off phones and computers and just find a quiet place to walk or sit and be still with myself and my thoughts. In the quiet, I find clarity. Sometimes, this place of peace takes a few minutes to find; other times, it takes days.

In times of trouble, she reaches out to those she loves and asks for help. She prefers her friends to show up, hold her hand and wrap their arms around her as she sheds tears. So, when Misti knew something had taken place in my life, she wanted to be there for me. Over time, I have been able to explain that when things get overwhelming for me, I need space and that my radio silence during tough emotional times doesn't say anything about how I feel for her.

One reason Misti and I have so much to teach each other is the tension of being mirrors for each other, and, in many ways, also complete opposites. Just as I have something to teach her about quiet, she teaches me about being needed. In the earlier moments of our friendship, it was difficult for me. It was overwhelming to feel so "needed" whenever something difficult took place in her life. But something about Misti always wins me over – maybe the intense courage she shows in her vulnerability. I always come back to this thought: "Wow! This woman is so freakin' brave! She actually knows how to ask for help."

Over the years, I have grown to appreciate more and more her way of being. She has challenged me to come outside of the "cave" when I have pondered my feelings and decisions far too long. She has helped me realize that there have been moments in my life when I crossed over the line from creating quiet space to hear and feel my instincts to running away from making tough decisions. She has also taught me the importance of facing the challenges head on and sharing my insecurities and fears with others so they can help resolve the difficult issues at hand. It takes bravery to show up in the world the way she so boldly shines – demanding what she needs and deserves in life.

My sincere admiration for Misti's vulnerable courage leads me to always call her back, to text her words of encouragement from time to time, and to show up at her doorstep to hold her hand or just let her scream, ponder or cry it all out. I'd like to learn how to embody her magnetic paradox, being equally scared and brave at the same time.

Alfred North Whitehead says that beauty requires contrasts held in tension, and beyond all the things we can teach each other, the beauty of my friendship with Misti rests in the tension created by our differences, and by our ability to understand and allow each other to be exactly who she is.

One Sunday afternoon, several years into our friendship, Misti asked me over to lunch. Francesca, her life partner, was on a camping trip with her father, so we had the place to ourselves. After dinner, as we sat at the dining room table, Misti said, "Mali, can we talk about something that has to do with our friendship?"

"Oh, boy," I thought. "I don't like the sound of this."

Aloud I said, "Sure. What's up?"

"Well, I guess my feelings are a bit hurt."

Pause.

"What did I do to hurt your feelings, Misti?"

Pause.

"That's just it, Mali. It's what you don't do. There are times when I am really upset about something and I need a friend. When I reach out to you, it takes you hours, sometimes days, to call me back. Sometimes I don't feel like you care that much about me or my feelings. I feel like I'm always there for you – even when you don't ask. I guess I wish you would do the same for me."

I sat back in my chair, quietly processing all that she had just thrown out there. To her, the seconds felt like hours. "Can you please say something?" she said. "I'm feeling a little uncomfortable with the silence."

Ah-hah! A smile came over my face. "I think we have just helped each other figure this all out, Misti," I said. "You see, I love the silence when my heart and mind are confronted with chaos. I need to sit back and process when I feel uncomfortable about things that are presented to me. I just realized that we are polar opposites when it comes to handling similar situations, and now, your way of being and processing totally makes sense to me."

She leaned in slightly across the table, inviting me to continue.

"Most of my life, I've been surrounded by people," I explained. "I grew up in a small apartment with seven people. I had to share a bedroom with two sisters until college. When I wanted to have a quiet space and stillness, there weren't many places I could run and hide. As an adult, I deeply value space and freedom – that sense of calm. My 'quiet' time is sacred to me. It's not about running from my problems, or from the people I love. It's not that I don't want or need your support. But first and most importantly, I need to hear myself think and feel with clarity.

I guess it comes down to me sharing what works best for me, and listening to you share what works for you. I promise to do better at being there for you when you need me, so long as you agree to provide me the quiet space I need to process during my difficult or stressful time."

Pause. I reached for her hands. Her eyes welled up with tears, and I knew that she got it! At that moment, we understood each other better as human beings, as friends and as sisters. I continued: "One of the most beautiful things our friendship has taught me is that we don't all express need, love, pain or joy in the same way. It doesn't mean we don't feel all those things. And it doesn't mean I don't care for someone who is different than I am, or love that person."

"I love you, sis," Misti said. She smiled and squeezed my hands … and then let out a huge, disgusting burp. We laughed so hard we couldn't breathe, especially after a rich meal of sticky rice and coconut salmon (Misti's favorite dish from my repertoire).

Through the give and take, the push and pull of our friendship, Misti has taught me about unconditional love and acceptance. We give this to one another as we continually negotiate our differences, but she has also taught me to give it to myself, to love all my bruised and broken pieces. Misti is like a deeply loyal and rambunctious elephant pushing me across the many rivers in life. At the same time, she helps me to see the firefly, all the fireflies, within me.

"Shift"

All I was
All I am
Dark nights fading
Bright skies await
Shake me to open my eyes.

Slowly – surely
I feel alive.

Soft earth caresses my feet
Water, no longer beneath
Light blue clouds starting to lift
I spread my wings –
Time ... has allowed me to shift.

PART VIII

CONCLUSION:
PEACE AND
THE WRITING LIFE

Why I Write

When I was 12 years old, recurring dreams of the night we escaped Laos helped me to understand that life experiences, even the most meaningful ones, can be repressed and lost forever. This realization motivated me to journal as much as possible, because I wanted to have a record of places I had been, people I had known and lessons I had learned. This desire to honor the moments and encounters in my life gave birth to my writing.

Even in my early days of journaling, my words did not just capture the details of everyday life. Rather than straightforward accounts of my days, my writing came to me in the form of poetry. As a young girl, rhymes came very easily. As I matured, so did my writing. My poetry no longer needed to rhyme. The poems simply needed to flow through me.

The process of inspiration and creation remains a mystery in which I participate by showing up and remaining present. I never write unless I am inspired. My inspiration usually shows up with a tingling in my fingertips, and from there, emotions take over. That's when I know to grab a pen and paper or place my fingers on a keyboard.

My first published piece was called, "I Came on my Own." My ninth-grade teacher, Mrs. Cartwright, gave us an assignment that required creative writing. I turned in a piece from my journal, a piece about the need to have a sense of belonging. Mrs. Cartwright had me stay after class and asked if I actually wrote the piece. I told her that it was from my journal.

"My dear, this is not a typical journal entry," she said. "This is what we call poetry. In my 17-year teaching career, I have never known a ninth grader to write such a descriptive and powerfully mature piece. I want to enter it in an amateur poetry contest."

My face lit up with delight. I said, "Mrs. Cartwright, if you think it's good enough to submit . . . ."

"It's more than good enough."

Three months later, I received a letter stating that Iliad Press had selected my poem, "I Came on My Own," for publication in their anthology.

◇◇

"I Came On My Own"
I came on my own.
Forced to leave by a society in which I did not belong,
ignored by another that did not want me,
I ran without shoes to protect my feet
and arrived without strength to protect my soul.
I had nowhere else to go,
so I continued forward; with every step
I was weakened by those who crossed my path.
I tripped; I fell.
Without touching me, they cut my hair,
and beat my face beyond recognition.

I allowed it to happen; I knew no other way.
I was only thankful to be alive.

I come on my own.
My journey has no end.
I do not search for any particular place.
I have no home; I do not belong anywhere or to anyone.
My hands are not clean.
I come on my own.
I stopped at a playground and sat on the swings,
the sun warm upon my skin.
A child came to me and offered me something to drink.
I smiled and touched his hands gently.
I did not speak the language, but he understood
my words without words.
I sipped the water from his cup and gave it back;
I closed my eyes for a brief second
and opened them to watch the child leave in his mother's arms.

CONCLUSION: PEACE AND THE WRITING LIFE **167**

✳ ✳ ✳

For years, I walked, alone,
without being offered anything to drink.
I only knew to steal and fight to stay alive.
I was so hungry it hurt to breathe.
I held back my tears until I could no longer see.
I came on my own.
Someone ran toward me just before I hit the ground.
It nearly took my death for you to save my life.
Remembering back to the day I arrived in your world,
if you knew then that my death was inevitable;
if I had stayed in the place from where I came
would you have saved me then?
Would you have carried me here?
Did I have to fall so hard?

◇◇◇

All through school, I continued to fill up my journals, sometimes writing two or three pieces a day. And I have continued to do so as an adult. Sometimes I write to simply relieve the pain and stress. Other times writing proves to be cathartic and/or healing. When I am going through difficult times, the words flow through me much more easily. Sometimes the tingling takes place when a pang of emotion hits.

Sadness, fear, anxiety, insecurity – any jolt to my heart sends stronger vibrations to my fingertips, and I must find some way to release the intensity. In my happier moments, I am able to write, but the tingling sensations through my fingers travel less frequently. Graham Greene touches on this mystery in his novel *The End of the Affair*: "Pain is easy to write. In pain, we are all dribble. What can one write about happiness?"

By the time I was 27 years old, I had written more than 400 pieces. After Chris passed away, I submitted the poem "Christopher," and it was selected by the International Society of Poets as one of the best poems of 2005. I was selected as one of the best poets, both in 2005 and again in 2007. In 2007, I was nominated as best Poet of the Year and my mother and I traveled to Las Vegas for the convention. This nomination was just what I needed to convince me that my writing was something worth sharing with the world. My father had been gone for a year, but he was with me too. I felt his presence deeply as I looked out into the audience and saw my mother smiling at me from the crowd.

Writing has always been a wonderful, natural "home" for me. I never focused on it as a career; rather, writing was always a place for me go when I felt I had nowhere, or no one else, to turn to.

While making friends is not difficult for me, there are moments when the energy of friends and family burden me. Though our love for each other never falters, I often struggle with having to "be OK" so others won't worry about me. At times, I need to step away from the outside world, from my family and friends, and go to a place much closer to my core, closer to nature, to the Universe, to all the gods and to the Almighty Power. My meditations and writing allow me to get to that place, to feel authentically what is really going on underneath all my layers and to work through my pain, worries and fears. Through each word and poem, I somehow release all the negative energy that once flowed through my body.

In essence, writing imbues my resident elephant, no stranger to grief, with a freeing lightness. When I write, her weight becomes lighter on my chest and she no longer lumbers through my days. Instead, she steps lightly, almost as if she is dancing.

It was not until I began the process of writing this book that I realized a career in writing is perfectly and naturally aligned with my life's purpose – my true innate purpose that is. I have instinctually known my whole life that my job was to emotionally support others when difficult things happen in life. I have grown to understand and appreciate how others value the ease with which I express deep thoughts and emotions, especially through my words.

The more I delved inward to capture the emotions that surfaced in every joyous and painful story I have recounted in this book, the closer I came to uncovering my true self. I have always been an artist, a creative soul. My life's journey, however, forced me to believe that in order to survive, I needed to use my left brain more than my right. I always held onto my creative self, but for most of my life, I have restricted those talents to a hobby.

This book has taken me through a deeper sense of healing than all the group therapy and independent counseling I have ever sought. It has helped me to reveal what truly excites and inspires me. It has taken me to the depths of my inner child and opened up new points of view for my adult self to consider. My inner being is most at peace when I write. This revelation and acceptance is the reason that, after seven years of protecting lives and offering others and myself a strong sense of structure and financial stability, I decided to trust in my true purpose and allow the journey to take me to even more extraordinary places.

A Million Fireflies was supposed to be about releasing all the lessons I have captured through my relationships, life experiences and repressed emotions. In the end, it became the catalyst for me to set my own self free to gift the world with my inner light – and follow my passion. In early 2011, I formed Mali Creative, LLC, to help others express their powerful messages and say what they feel is important to share with the world.

A Million Fireflies opened up my world to all the possibilities for my life's vision. I am a writer, and my heart feels most at peace when I am writing. So, I am redesigning my life so that I can make a living doing what I love most in life.

Never Alone

One irony of the writing life is that while solitude is required, being creative can often feel lonely. I have so much I want to express. I feel deeply, see things in vibrant colors and wear my heart on my sleeve. But I've learned that hearing about my raw emotions can make some people uncomfortable. My friends often exclaim, "You are too much!"

My friends don't say this in a negative way, but I hear it so often that I must assume people just don't get me sometimes. I always suspected there were other people out there like me, who would understand the depth of my emotions and see the same vibrancy in life that I do. "Perhaps if I found them," I often thought, "I would feel less alone in the world as an artist." I started going to poetry readings after college but never felt confident enough to read my own work. I loved the energy of coffee-house poetry nights. Everyone was so alive and vibrant, able to listen and share their points of view with others in the room. I love that about artists. Writing brings me home, and I always feel at home surrounded by other writers.

In May of 2010, I received an e-mail from a Lao-American writer and poet, Bryan Thao Whorra, who resides in Minnesota. I knew of him through the Lao community and from the connections I made as fundraising chairperson for the Lao Heritage Foundation. Bryan was organizing the first-ever Lao-American Writer's Summit, to be held in Minnesota during early August, and was writing to ask if I would be interested in participating. He was hoping, he said, to have 10 to 15 participants make history with this first summit, honoring the voice of Laos.

I was truly honored to receive the request but curious about the selection process. I asked how he knew of me and my work. As it turned out, he had been reading my poetry and postings on Facebook and also received recommendations from other summit coordinators and leaders within the Lao Community. When I did some online research, I realized he'd be commenting on and featuring my work on his blog about Lao writers for the past two years. I immediately accepted the honor.

August came quickly, and before I knew it, the plane landed. I ran into Na Bounheng, another participant, community leader, and a family friend, in baggage claim. We embraced and went out to the departure area to wait for the conference interns to pick us up and whisk us off to our hotel, an inn called The Loft. All expenses were paid, and I felt like a celebrity in many ways. It was quite a new experience. That evening, all the artists, as well as the summit coordinators, met up at a nearby Thai restaurant to officially kick off the Summit.

The evening was so colorful. Lao-American artists traveled from across the nation to be part of this historic event. As I looked around the table, I got emotional. I had read about some of these artists, seen a few of them in films and heard others' lyrics over the years. Some of them I hadn't heard of, but once I listened to their bios, it was humbling. For example, Bryan Thao Worra, author of *On The Other Side Of The Eye, Touching Detonations and Winter Ink,* is the first Lao-American to receive a Fellowship in Literature from the United States government's National Endowment for the Arts. And writer-director Thavisouk Phrasavath, Emmy Award winner, was nominated for the 2009 Academy Award and Film Independent Spirit Award. I felt even more honored to have been selected.

We toasted that night to this momentous experience, the first symposium of its kind, and promised to support future events for Lao artists.

The Summit was one of the most powerful experiences for me as a writer. More than winning any international poetry award, this experience truly gave me that strong sense of belonging I had been missing as an artist. It was impossible to feel alone surrounded by other Lao-American writers who shared very similar struggles with identity and growing up in poverty. I was greeted non-stop for three days by people I had never met. They embraced me, knew my name, spoke of specific poems I wrote and told me how I gave their emotions a voice. It was a truly humbling and wonderful experience to realize how I was showing up in their world and inspiring them. They valued my work as a writer and congratulated me for my bravery in sharing.

Before the Summit, I never fully accepted that I had anything special to offer when it came to my writing. I knew that my passion for it made my work more than a hobby and that somehow I had gotten good at it. But these people, relative strangers, saw more of my artistic gifts than I saw in myself – and helped me understand the impact of my words.

The most poignant moment took place on the last night of the Summit. All the artists had five to 10 minutes to perform or read our work to the audience. I had a collection of poems prepared, ones I had read multiple times at poetry readings back in D.C. but I woke up that morning knowing that what I prepared was not what I was meant to share that evening. Instead, I kept having visions of me holding a book on stage. I decided to print out excerpts from this book, which was still in the early production stage.

When it was my turn to take the stage, I told the audience that I had decided just that morning to step outside of my comfort zone and present pieces I hadn't shared with any other audience – three selections from my upcoming book.

As I read, I could see the impact of my writing on the attendees' faces – smiles, tears and laughter, the gamut of human emotion. I was in my element and felt for the first time an overwhelming sense of peace and calm about my book and sharing my stories. There were no spotlights that night, but spiritually, they were on, beaming a powerful, warm light from up above. As I continued to read, the light radiated from my body toward the audience, like the way fireflies light up in a chain reaction across a summer meadow. I could see all the faces, intently listening and reacting to every single syllable that escaped my lips. I heard the silent sighs as I shared my journey of healing; others seemed to remember themselves and lived out their emotions right alongside me. I spent years with that crowd of souls in those 10 minutes. For a brief time, we joined in this journey together.

I finished reading the last piece, and the audience erupted with applause. Little white flags of Kleenex flashed as people wiped away tears to reveal supportive smiles. As I left the stage, a lady in the front row stretched out her hands, and I reached for them. She squeezed my hands to show how proud she was of me. I sat down, overwhelmed by the generous support, and sought that silent inner place, grounding myself to be present with the performances that followed.

At closing time, a young lady with deep, brown eyes and a gentle presence came up to me and said, "Mali, you read tonight the words I have been searching for all my life. I, too, lost my father recently, and it has been hard to find others who truly understand what we go through when we lose those so dear to us. You have found the words to give me a voice. You helped me tonight by taking away feelings of isolation. I am not the only one in the world to feel such deep pain, am I?"

I squeezed both of her hands in mine, and we embraced as the tears (and mascara) rolled down her cheeks. "No, you are not the only one," I told her. "You are never alone."

I came home after that trip knowing an important truth about myself. I finally believed myself to be a real, legitimate, gifted writer. Though I didn't realize it, my joy, grief and loneliness have honed me into a fine instrument. I have always been designed to be a writer with a deeper purpose than I ever imagined.

The fireflies of Laos shine their light all over the world in the voices and work of all those who dare to share their gifts. As a writer, I aim to provide a voice for millions of others, giving birth to the million fireflies that will light up the darkest, most forsaken nights and remind the world that the land of a million elephants has grown the wings to rise above any tragedy.

"Let Go and Be"

I am trying to recall how many times
I sat like this underneath the stars
Held conversations with you from afar.

My life is beautiful –
With you here, with you there.

This heart has been exercised,
Instincts more sound than ever before
I realize now, you never left my side
Leading me to places of wonder –
exploration within and across the shores.

I hear you in the sunshine,
alongside moonless nights
Your laughter echoes louder than the sea
My vision is clear; this heart feels alive and free
The time has come ... let go ... BE.

How the Universe Keeps Me Writing

In October of 2007, one year after my father passed, I made plans to go on a writing trip with my friends, Misti and Steve, at a beach house owned by Misti's friend, Rita. We all had projects we needed to focus on. Misti was completing her first book. Steve planned to work on content for his business newsletters and website. And I wanted to finally pull all my poetry and short essays together to start the process of publishing my poetry book. We were to leave on a Thursday morning and return the following Monday.

The week before our trip, I was on the phone with my mother and asked how she was feeling with the one-year anniversary of Paw's passing coming up so soon. She grew quiet and asked me, "Is it supposed to feel this way? Is it supposed to feel this empty inside still?" I sat there, silent, and I could feel the tears flowing down her face from across the phone. I couldn't believe it. Our roles were completely reversed. There I was, her daughter, who had also experienced the deep loss of her partner, trying to console my mother.

"You have had 33 years of your life with him by your side," I told her. "You will be missing him this deeply for a long while and you will continue to miss him always." I cried as I thought about Chris and my father. "Mom, I don't have to go on this writing trip, you know. I can stay here this weekend to be with you as we prepare for the memorial ceremony."

She quickly replied, "No, I'll be fine, and we can take care of things when you get back. Your father would want you to go on with your dreams. He knows your writing is important to you. Go."

"No, Mai. I want to stay and be with you. I'll see you this weekend."

That night, I called my friends to let them know I was not going. They were both very disappointed but did their best to sound supportive. I hung up the phone feeling guilty.

I lay in bed that night with many thoughts running through my head. My mother was experiencing so much pain, and I wondered if I had the strength to get her through her emotions when I was struggling so many with my own. I prayed to the Universe that the heaviness would lift and wished that my father didn't have to leave us so soon.

That night, I experienced something very similar to the dream sequence I had when Chris passed away. The same vividness of colors, and the sounds and smells of nature – all of it was coming at me again in another dream sequence – this time with messages about my father.

I was standing upon sand with a little boy resting on my right hip. We were looking out into the distance, beyond the ocean water, watching brown mountain ranges. All of the sudden, hundreds of pores formed on the mountains, opening up to release hundreds upon hundreds of parrots. There were parrots of every color, shape and size.

The next thing the child and I noticed were the yellow parrots breaking off from the group and flying closer and closer together to form an object. The child on my hip said, "Look, it's the shape of the sun." I nodded. After that, the parrots gathered to form a different object. "Wow," exclaimed the child. "A rainbow!" I smiled in awe and nodded. Finally, the white birds gathered together, and the little boy screamed, "Eew! What's that?"

I laughed and calmly replied, "It might be an octopus, since it has tentacles."

Then, the parrots all flew closer to form a cluster, and the flock flew away toward the west … all the birds but one. A turquoise parrot stayed behind and flew toward us. I watched as it spread its wings and headed in our direction. It gently glided over our heads and landed behind me on top of a building. I turned my body slightly to follow the bird and suddenly noticed thousands of people standing behind me and the child, witnessing what we were witnessing.

The turquoise parrot landed on a few of their shoulders, softly jumping from one person to the next until it landed gently on my right shoulder. I rubbed its beak against my cheek, and when I turned to look at it, I saw my father's eyes looking back at me.

Tears rushed down my face, and the parrot continued to rub its beak. "Thank you for being with me when I was dying," it said (*he* said). "Thank you for taking good care of me. Thank you for loving me. It's time to fly." I woke up, reached for the phone and called Mai. At the end of my descriptive explanation of the dream, my mother became convinced that my father wanted me to go on the writing trip.

Two days later, Misti, Steve and I headed down to North Carolina's Outer Banks. We were all so excited. As we made the drive, Misti asked what made me change my mind.

"I had a dream about my father," I said. "And it helped me to feel that he is still here, supporting me and wishing for me to move forward with my life. I believe he wants me to work on my book."

They asked me to tell them about the dream, and I described each detail I could remember. When I finished, there was silence. A few seconds later, Misti, who had visited the beach house before, said, "My hair is standing on end, and I have goose bumps all over. When we get to Rita's place, I'm going to give you the keys, Mali, and you go in first. Steve and I will wait in the car."

When we arrived, I unlocked the door and entered the house. Directly in front of me was a large, colorful painting. I could not believe my eyes when I saw vibrantly-colored parrots, all waiting to greet me. I felt the warmth of my father's smile. My tears flowed, and I smiled as I wiped them away and walked backed to the car.

Misti and Steve both embraced me. Misti warned us that the painting wasn't the only reason she was so moved by my story. As we placed our things inside Rita's beautiful beach home, we were awestruck by her passion for parrots. In fact, there were parrots *everywhere* – on dish towels, blankets, lamps, even martini glasses. All we could do was laugh.

When Misti called Rita to let her know we had arrived safely, she told Misti that she had something cool to show us. She directed us through the room and pointed out a wooden parrot statue. Steve was the first to locate it. When it caught my eye, my heart skipped a beat. The parrot statue was turquoise.

"Rita says to pull the tail, Steve," Misti shouted. My heart now began to race. The statue uttered in a parrot's tone, "I MISS YOU." I had to sit down. This was enough to convince Misti and Steve that my dream was more like a vision. It was enough to convince me.

The next couple of days were filled with words and raindrops. Sunday evening rolled by quickly, and we each felt a sense of accomplishment with our work. I had copied all the poems and short essays I wanted to include in my book and created a collection.

The sun finally broke through around 3:00 p.m., and although we had cloud covering most of the day, the rain had stopped. I was preparing dinner in the kitchen when Steve called us out on the dock behind Rita's house to watch the sun prepare to set. The breeze came to caress my face; I closed my eyes several times and just took deep breaths.

They stayed on the back porch while I went inside to check the oven. All of the sudden, I heard Misti open the back door to scream, "Mali, grab your camera; grab it quick!" I ran to my bedroom, got the camera and headed onto the porch. I snapped a shot, and as quickly as I saw it in front of the camera, it disappeared. A rainbow had formed in front of the setting sun.

"Do you both realize what just happened?" I asked, turning to Misti and Steve, astonished. "In my dream, the birds first formed the sun, and a rainbow followed." I took a deep breath. The tears came from within and silently rolled down my face. My friends and I just stood there until the sun had completely set beyond the water's edge.

Three hours later, we finished our dinner and walked out onto the dock, talking about our goals for our professional lives and our hopes for our romantic lives. We certainly laughed a lot that night. As Misti and Steve clowned around, climbing on pieces of wood they found or jumping on each other's backs, I decided to sit on the dock and dangle my feet toward the water. The moon was out, and the breeze was strong, chilling me to the bone. I thought about Chris. Docks tend to remind me of him, but this night, it was not in a tragic way. I felt close to him, connected to his higher spirit somehow. I closed my eyes, inhaled and whispered, "I haven't lost anything. You are always with me."

After a little while, I got up to join my friends. Suddenly, Misti pointed and started jumping up and down. "Eew!" she screamed. "What's that?"

I froze. I could not take another step. Those were the exact words the young boy spoke in my vision.

Steve's eyes grew large as he realized the same thing. He grabbed my hands and said, "She's pointing at all the jellyfish in the water. They have tentacles."

I jumped and started shaking off the energy. I found myself screaming now, "Oh my God. Oh my God." My friends were as astonished as I was; we all started jumping around trying to shake off the energy.

This was not the first time the Universe revealed myself to me, highlighting my connection to it through dreams. Three times before, I'd had dreams in which numbers revealed themselves to me. Using these numbers, my father, and then Chris, played the lottery and won significant amounts of money each time. But a lottery win of hundreds of dollars was worthless compared to this. I knew my dreams gave me visions, like my grandmother. But I wasn't prepared for this epiphany, this revelation of the true value of my work and my voice.

I don't know how, but I slept soundly that night. I finally embraced that I had perhaps a stronger spiritual connection than most people in the world. Instead of frightening me, it comforted me that night. I felt a sense of peace in accepting that I am tuned in to the spiritual laws of the Universe. I no longer needed to overanalyze or make excuses for the things I saw, felt and believed; I just had to trust that these gifts were for me to have and use in whatever way gave me the most internal peace.

The next morning, Steve volunteered to drive home. Two hours into our trip, our conversation dwindled, and we entered that comfortably-silent phase, each turned inward to his or her own thoughts. I turned my head to look out into the distance. It was perfect, late-October weather with somewhat cloudy skies.

My eyes traced the peaks and valleys of what appeared to be brown mountain ranges. I remembered the brown mountains in my vision (I could no longer call it a dream). As soon as I remembered, the hairs on my arms stood up, and as if from nowhere, hundreds upon hundreds of brown birds lifted off the ground and flew together toward the west.

I stopped breathing. I allowed my eyes to adjust and my being to somehow get centered before I started giggling. I didn't know what else to do with my pent-up energy. Misti turned around to ask what I was giggling about. I simply pointed out the window.

It took her a few seconds to see what I saw. In a very slow tone, she calmly said, "Oh my God. Steve, pull over when you can. There's no way this weekend is real."

He eventually found a safe place to pull over. We all gazed in silence at the flock of birds. I placed my hand on Steve's left shoulder, and he grabbed my hand. Misti took the other. I leaned my head upon the back of the driver's headrest, and we all turned our heads to follow the birds' flight westward. We watched until they disappeared from view.

I did not have a dream of parrots and my father's eyes. I had a vision of my reality being played out. I had a message from the Universe that simply wanted to remind me that those we love, once physically gone from us, are never far away from us spiritually. Their energy remains connected with us. They are always with us.

"A New Day"

Your presence reaches me like the sun,
shining on me through winter snow and rainy summer days
Nothing, not even time, will take your love away

My hopes extend beyond these dreams
I am awake every moment – you bring me to life
Nothing compares to being next to you through the stillness of nights

These waking moments, I savor them with each breath
My heart – free like wildflowers being sprinkled by the endless clouds
I am more in love with life than ever – singing my heart out loud

Your embrace takes my breath away, pulls me like the moonbeams,
lighting up the darkest of evening skies
To the millions of teardrops that once fell from these eyes …
I wave the sweetest farewell as they float away like fireflies.

Like fireflies … starting a new day.

"From All Sides Now"

I am here –
a new person that glows
and sees the world in revolving colors.
Once dark and gray,
my nights now brighten up
with the moonlight's reminder.
This heart CAN love again –
without the force of winds or rain,
without the pressures
of those wanting to protect their sweet flower.

I hear whispers in my dreams,
telling me I am free to live; I am free to fly.
With all the wonders this life has for me to discover –
how can I possibly remain silent and still?

I am running now
like never before,
expressing my words, revealing my heart –
no longer afraid to simply BE.

I taste each breath,
like sweet fruit lingering upon my lips.
I capture each image –
like a photograph
I will never erase from my heart
I look at love from all sides now –
my past, my present, my future
What was still is and what will be
shall come to reveal itself in time.

You are here now, by my side.
I wish to carry you along,
as far as our journeys will allow it,
and if you wish to stay, I will not argue.
I will no longer fight to suppress
the pitter patter of my newly beating heart ...
And yes, I do love you
as you have come to love me –
without judgment, without pretense, without fear.

A Field of Fireflies Opened My Eyes

I stared out into the stillness of the night. It was 9:45 p.m. on a Friday night in May of 2007, and I was not quite sure how I came to be out beyond the lights of the city, in Catlett, Virginia, at the Lao-Buddhist Temple my father helped build. Though tears had dried up, my eyes still throbbed. I could be with my friends at a club downtown. When they called me earlier that evening for happy hour, I was still finishing up at work. I told them I might join them later.

My heart had been heavy all day. I woke up feeling that way. Sometimes that still happens.

It was early spring, and the evening air chilled me. The dogwoods were in bloom, and trees were budding with lime-green leaves waking up from the dark, cold winter. On the way home from work, I heard a song on the radio: "By Your Side" by Sade. My heart reacted in a way it hadn't in a very long time. It caved in. This was supposed to be the song for my first dance as Chris's wife. I was four years removed from when my wedding was supposed to take place, but I continued to be haunted by the lyrics:

> *You think I'd leave your side baby?*
> *You know me better than that.*
> *You think I'd let you down when you're down on your knees?*
> *I wouldn't do that.*

Sitting there in commuter traffic, tears poured from my eyes. Images ran through my mind; one by one, I saw images of Chris's face, Chester's smile, then Mac's grin, followed by Peter's embrace, and then finally my father's eyes. Four years – so many deep heartbreaks. Why?

When I finally got home, the tears continued to flow. I turned off the engine and sat in front of my dark, empty condo, physically frozen, unable to exit the car. My heart was beating rapidly; the tears could not be tamed. Filled with sadness, I could hear my internal self asking over and over, "Why? Why? Why?"

I sat there, my fingers toying with the car keys, and decided to go for a ride. I didn't know where I was going; I just knew I needed to clear my mind and relieve my heart. Perhaps a long drive would do me good. I headed west toward the Shenandoah Valley. An hour later, I stepped out of the car to find myself on the grounds of the Lao-Buddhist Temple.

My father's and Chris's memorial stones were there, both beyond the man-made lake. I walked toward the water, planning to sit near those stones and spiritually connect with the physical objects. Maybe then, I could know for sure that my beloved ones could still be reached, that I could "touch" them somehow.

I didn't even get close to the lake. As I made my way down a gravel road so dark that I could barely see my black shoes on the surface, my forehead felt a soft brush, like a kiss of tiny wings. I stopped and closed my eyes.

When I opened them again, I saw a few flashes of light in front of me. I blinked again. There were more flashes of light. I didn't quite understand what I was seeing until I stood completely still and focused my vision beyond my nose.

As my perspective expanded, goose bumps spread across my body. In the middle of this gravel road, between my car and the moon-lit lake, without trees or bushes to block my view of the open sky, I was surrounded by what looked like a million fireflies.

I could not laugh nor cry. I simply lifted my arms and began to slowly turn in circles. Fireflies were everywhere. To say there were at least a million of them is not a stretch. The landscape sparkled with their flickering messages.

These things can happen in the Universe, in *my* Universe. My losses pulled me here to this sacred place of wonder in the first place. Without them, I would never have had the opportunity to dance inside of this most beautiful and cherished moment. My father, Chris, Rafael and everyone else who graced me with love and wisdom, are leading and will continue to lead me to places of awe and magic, places where I can feel that no one who has truly loved me has ever left my side. Energy lives on. Life sees the souls from which energy ignites, like the spark of a firefly.

I stood there with the earth beneath my feet, the moon and stars above, love and life continuing, my doubts and fears being lifted by a million fireflies.

There was no longer a need to search for the memorial stones. I had what I needed. The fireflies that evening were the Universe's gentle reminder to trust in things that are hard to believe, things that others may never understand.

I walked toward my car and made my way home as light and as bright as a firefly.

✳ ✳ ✳

Acknowledgements

This book has been a five-year journey. I don't know if
A Million Fireflies would have ever come to life without the
support of the amazing people who have been part of this journey
with me.

The structure, flow and richness of poetic storytelling inside
this book would not be what it is without the support of Leslee
Johnson and Taylor Mallory, my brilliantly-talented editors. Their
professionalism, flexibility and passion for the success of our book
made all the difference in the world. Thank you for helping me
to see my own light and bravery so that I could release my million
fireflies!

Norasack Pathammavong, my friend and soul brother, is
responsible for the design and layout of the book. I am in awe
of his creative genius. He is one of the most generous people I
know. His commitment to helping others live out their dreams
inspires me. Thank you, Brother! Thank you to the entire
Norasack Design team.

The following women (and gentleman) served on my advisory
committee for the book launch: Kristina Bouweiri, Vannessa
Calderon, Linda Cureton, Cynthia De Lorenzi, Kelly Harman,
Steven Thomas and Kim Russo. Thank you for your invaluable
insight and commitment to being on this journey with me!

My official reviewers spent many hours reading the manuscript
and offering their feedback to make it more powerful. They are:
Mina Mounkhaty, Niphasone and Xai Souphom, Karin Tovar, Debi
Wheatley, Peter Pereyra, Marisol Flamenco, and Claudia Paulsen
Young. Thank you for your love and support!

Finally, I would like to thank my mother and father, Keonoukane and Sivone Phonpadith, my grandmother, Khamkong, my siblings, Mina, Lola, Soudara, my brother-in-law, Ong, Christopher Meehan (in memorial), Bill "Pops" and the Meehan family, the Beckford and Rubio families, the Mounkhaty, Saykhamphone, Vichith, Khamvongsa, Souvandara, Phrasavang, and Sengchanh families, the Rajapakse and Reddy families, the McCarty family, the Douangmala, Inversin, Senthavong, Chiasone, Abuan, and Tichawonna families, Lao Heritage Foundation, Davies Unitarian Church, Wat Lao Buddhavong, Ajahn Noumy, Misti Burmeister, Yvette Nash, Monalisa Arias, Vernice Armour, Steve Dorfman, Maggie Robledo, Masoud and Paolla Edalatkhah, Tony Marciante, Peter Pereyra, Karin Tovar, Marisol Flamenco, Alex Alburqueque, Limary Suarez, Damiana Astudillo, Paul Montesano, Julia Samuels, Margarita Rozenfeld, Amra Alirejsovic, Vannasone Keodara, Bounchanh Mouangkham, Bryan Thao Whorra, Thavisouk Phrasavath, Maimah Karmo, Richa Badami, Amy Horn, Matthew Lau, Pierre Mege, Nucky Walder, Mario Marcel, Marcela Ferlito Walder, Regis Arnone, John Chia, Brian Winters, Iris Saltzman, Ira Peppercorn, Dede Haas, Mike Hincewicz, Debbie Gallo, Dreva Esparza, Victoria Staudinger, Rafael Beckford (in memorial), and all of the other supportive and loving friends I wish I could mention on these pages. Thank you for your encouragement and providing me the safe space to create and share my world with you, and now with others. You are all my inspiring fireflies!

About Mali Phonpadith

 Mali Phonpadith, a poet, author and entrepreneur, was born in Laos during the Vietnam War. Her family fled across the Mekong River on a boat and made it safely to the refugee camps of Ubon Rachatani in Thailand.

Mali and her family arrived in the United States when she was five years old. Twelve years later, her first poem, "I Came on my Own," was published by Iliad Press. Soon after, "Unselfish Love," "This Feeling," "Christopher," "My Days," "For Granted," "Peter's Sky" and "New York's Embrace" were published by several internationally-recognized affiliates of The International Society of Poets and The London Press. And in 2007, Mali was nominated Best Poet of the Year by The International Society of Poets.

In her forthcoming release, A Million Fireflies, Phonpadith takes us on a journey of love and loss, incorporating both poetry and her real-life stories to give voice to the true language of a heart that has seen much, felt deeply and survived to shine.

Mali Phonpadith resides in Virginia, USA, and is CEO of Mali Creative, LLC, a marketing and communications firm that helps entrepreneurs and community leaders effectively market their core values and win over the attention of their target audiences.